Mary Bateson

A Collection of original Letters from the Bishops to the Privy council

1564

Mary Bateson

A Collection of original Letters from the Bishops to the Privy council 1564

ISBN/EAN: 9783337130824

Printed in Europe, USA, Canada, Australia, Japan

Cover: Foto ©ninafisch / pixelio.de

More available books at **www.hansebooks.com**

THE CAMDEN MISCELLANY,

VOLUME THE NINTH:

CONTAINING

VISITATIONS OF CHURCHES IN THE PATRONAGE OF ST. PAUL'S CATHEDRAL.

"THE SPOUSELLS" OF THE PRINCESS MARY, 1508.

A COLLECTION OF ORIGINAL LETTERS FROM THE BISHOPS TO THE PRIVY COUNCIL, 1564.

PAPERS RELATING TO THOMAS WENTWORTH, FIRST EARL OF STRAFFORD.

HAMILTON PAPERS. ADDENDA.

MEMOIRS OF NATHANIEL, LORD CREWE.

THE JOURNAL OF MAJOR RICHARD FERRIER, M.P., 1687.

PRINTED FOR THE CAMDEN SOCIETY.
M.DCCC.XCV.

COUNCIL OF THE CAMDEN SOCIETY
FOR THE YEAR 1894-5.

President.

THE RIGHT HON. THE EARL OF CRAWFORD, K.T., LL.D., F.R.S., &c., &c.

JAMES J. CARTWRIGHT, ESQ., M.A., F.S.A., *Treasurer.*
REV. J. SILVESTER DAVIES, M.A., F.S.A.
REV. J. WOODFALL EBSWORTH, M.A., F.S.A.
JAMES GAIRDNER, ESQ., *Secretary.*
SAMUEL RAWSON GARDINER, ESQ., M.A., LL.D., *Director.*
REV. F. A. GASQUET, D.D.
DAVID HANNAY, ESQ.
REV. WILLIAM HUNT, M.A.
ARTHUR W. HUTTON, ESQ., M.A.
J. BASS MULLINGER, ESQ., M.A.
REV. CHARLES NEIL, M.A.
J. E. L. PICKERING, ESQ.
H. C. SOTHERAN, ESQ.
HENRY R. TEDDER, ESQ.
PERCY M. THORNTON, ESQ., M.P.

Talbot. *See* Shrewsbury
Talbot, Sir Gilbert, deputy of Calais, 5
Thames, the river, 8
Theimseke, George de, provost of Cassel, 4
Toison d'Or, king-at arms, 4
Tournaments, 25-29

Wales, prince of. *See* Henry
———, princess of. *See* Katharine

Walhain, John de Berghes, seigneur de, 5
Warham, William, archbishop of Canterbury, lord chancellor, 7, 10, 11, 20
West, Dr. Nicholas (afterwards bishop of Ely), 6
Winchester, bishop of. *See* Fox, Richard
Worcester, bishop of. *See* Giglis, John de

A COLLECTION OF ORIGINAL LETTERS

FROM

THE BISHOPS TO THE PRIVY COUNCIL,

1564,

WITH RETURNS OF THE JUSTICES OF THE PEACE AND OTHERS WITHIN THEIR RESPECTIVE DIOCESES, CLASSIFIED ACCORDING TO THEIR RELIGIOUS CONVICTIONS.

EDITED BY

MARY BATESON.

PRINTED FOR THE CAMDEN SOCIETY.
MDCCCXCIII.

PREFACE.

In the calendar of the MSS. of the Marquis of Salisbury, Part I., p. 306 (No. 1024), will be found a brief summary of the contents of a MS. preserved at Hatfield House (pressmark, c. c. 5), which contains the replies sent by the archbishops and bishops to questions put to them by the Privy Council in a letter of October 17, 1564. This letter is not now known to be extant, but from the answers of the bishops it appears that they were asked to classify those who were already justices of the peace according as they were favourable, indifferent, or hostile to the proceedings of the Government in matters of religion, and also to name the persons who in their opinion were fit to be put into office and those who should be removed from office. To this end they were asked to consult those of the leading men of their dioceses who were favourable to the Government, and with their help to make suggestions for the remedying of disorders, for the fuller repression of popery, maintenance of justice, promotion of God's gospel, and punishment of those who afflicted the honest and godly and maintained the perverse and ungodly. As the same method is not adopted by each bishop it is difficult to tabulate the results with accuracy; roughly estimated, the total of justices marked favourable is 431; marked indifferent, neuter, or not favourable, 264; hinderers or adversaries, 157. The dioceses reported to be most hostile to the Government were those of the north and west; Carlisle, Durham, York, Worcester, Hereford, and Exeter were strong in opposition. Staffordshire was troubled by a knot of "hinderers" led by the Vernons, and in Buckinghamshire Sir Robert Drury, Sir Robert Peckham, and Sir William Dormer were the leaders of a large band of men "not fit to be trusted." Where the towns are mentioned these are found to be in nearly every case more hostile to the Government than the counties. Newcastle-on-Tyne alone is an exception.

These lists serve as a measure of the progress which the doctrines of the Reformation had made among the middle classes, for the administrators of local government are here classified as they supported or opposed the doctrines of the Church of Rome; the bishops were not as yet concerned to exclude the advanced reformers from office, and there is nothing in these lists to show that they included among the men " not fit to be trusted " any persons other than those who were reputed to have leanings towards Roman Catholicism. These lists should prove valuable to local historians, for they give a complete religious census of the leading men of each county. Most of the names may be identified in the large county histories, but as a rule genealogical evidence alone is here forthcoming; the bishops' remarks give to many a distinct political and religious identity.

It would be interesting to trace the results which attended the Council's efforts to secure a body of justices willing to carry out its wishes, but this cannot be done with any completeness until the lists of justices of the peace, which may be found on the backs of the Patent Rolls, have been printed. So far as I have been able to compare these lists it does not appear that the Council effected any sudden changes; hinderers and persons not conformable sometimes remained in office, and signed the Act of Supremacy in 1569.[a] Several of the bishops were obliged to recommend the retention of the services of men who were "noted adversaries of religion," either by reason of their intimate acquaintance with the law or because they could not recommend any persons as fit to fill their places. The steady increase of the powers of the justices of the peace in religious matters which went on throughout the reign is proof enough that the Council found that it could secure the co-

[a] Eliz. D.S.P. lx. 22.

operation of this body. It was the Act of the preceding year (5 Eliz. c. i.) which necessitated an inquiry at this particular time, for the Council had begun a new system when not justices of assize only, but also justices of the peace, were made responsible within the limits of their commission for the execution of the Act for preserving the power of the Crown against the usurpation of the see of Rome.

Only favourers of religion and godly proceedings could afford to laugh with Falstaff at "Robert Shallow esquire," "in the county of Gloster justice of peace and *coram*," ay and *cust-alorum*, ay and *rato-lorum* too, "a gentleman who writes himself *armigero* on every bill, warrant, quittance, or obligation *armigero*," but men not staid in religion trembled when Robert Shallow esquire made a Star Chamber matter of their doings or let the Council know of them.

The same careful watch which the Council kept on justices of the peace was kept upon the corporations, especially when the aldermen were by their municipal privilege also justices of the peace. From lists like these the Council got the information which enabled it to decide who should be appointed as mayor, aldermen, and capital burgesses when charters of incorporation were to be granted or "confirmations" of old charters drawn up in which only the most important sentences of the originals were changed. Since the mayor, aldermen, and capital burgesses appointed in the first instance were to fill up all vacancies in their ranks by co-option, care had to be taken to avoid the appointment of adversaries of religion.*

These returns afford a most characteristic illustration of that infinite care for detail and love of minute inquiry which inspired

* Take for instance the charters granted to Leicester, 1588, 1599 (J Thompson, pp. 285 and 307); in the second the mayor, bailiffs, and burgesses are all named; so too at Newbury (Money, p. 228) in 1596, the mayor, six aldermen, and twenty-four capital burgesses are singled out by name; at Beverley (Poulson, p. 12) the charter of 15 Eliz. names the governors to be called the Common Council, they are to appoint to all vacancies. An interesting collection of cases of this kind might be made to illustrate the growth of oligarchy in English towns.

the Elizabethan Government. The lists of justices of the peace contain the great names of each county, for it was not beneath the dignity of a member of Her Majesty's Privy Council to sit at quarter sessions, but they also contain the names of many small men unskilled in the laws; all were watched with equal zeal by the Council's jealous eye; nobody could hope to keep his religious convictions a secret from the Council; however outwardly conformable, if inwardly he was frowardly superstitious the Council knew it. Matthew Parker alone shrinks from ticketing the religion of every man, and writes tartly when he sends the list of names commended to him for the dioceses of Llandaff and Oxford [a] that "what these be and what others be your honours of the Council know much better than we can inform you, and as for myself I know them not and sometime informers serve their own turn and gratify their friends." The remedies for disorders suggested by the bishops are the favourite remedies of the time and show no originality; they recommend those in authority to receive the communion frequently in order to set a good example, and to hear sermons and discourses before quarter sessions in order to keep their religious duties well in mind; oaths cannot be too frequently administered to suspected persons and to those in authority. The evil of privileged jurisdictions exempt from their control is one which several bishops were anxious to remove.

My best thanks are due to the Bishop of Peterborough, who drew my attention to this manuscript, and to Mr. R. T. Gunton, the Marquis of Salisbury's secretary, who kindly made arrangements for my convenience in copying it. Owing to the exigencies of space it has been found necessary to print the names in lines instead of in lists, and in some minor particulars to abandon the arrangement of the manuscript. Abbreviations are expanded, and square brackets used where the sense is doubtful.

MARY BATESON.

[a] Then vacant.

LETTERS FROM THE BISHOPS TO THE PRIVY COUNCIL, 1564.

1024. f. 1a. Press mark, c. c. 5.

My dutie humblie remembrid; your Lordships letters datid the xvii[th] of this instant I receavid the xx[th] of the same at night, and acording to my bounden dutie I haue with all diligencie traveiled to accomplishe your commaundement, and have herinclosed sent unto your honors a true Certificat aunswearing the Seuerall pointes of your lettres acordinglie. I thank god I am well acquainted with my flocke and namelie with the affections of such as be bell weathers and leaders of the Same. Sure I am I haue dealt faithfullie herin, for in this my report neather haue I fearid partis or respectid person but Simplie folowed a plaine truthe, vsing the aduise of Such as be zelous in religion, skillfull in the state of their Countreie and good members of the commenwealthe. Ffor Worcester Shire I vsed the Counsell of Sir Thomas Russell, knight, for the Citie of Worcester I vsed the Counsell of Christopher Dighton, a grave and a wise Citizin. Ffor the Towne of Warwick and that percell of my dioceses there I vsed the Counsell of William Huddisdon, gent, and Nicholas Jackson, person of Halford. I wold haue consulted with mo in this matter, but Such as I thought most meete for the purpose were out of the Countreie and men are loth to meddle in matters that may turne to their displeasure. The repressing of

diligentlie enquire of matters of religion and effectuouslie punishe transgressers of the Same.

Yf gentillmen and Such as be in auctoritie were Inyoined everie quarter once to receave the Communion and to heare a Sermon to the good example of others.

f. 1b.

Yf popishe and peruerse priestes which, misliking, religion haue forsaken the ministerie and yet liue in corners, are kept in gentillmens houses and had in greate estimacion with the people, where they marvailouslie pervert the Simple and blaspheme the truthe, were restrainid of their libertie & put to the othe for the quenes Maiesties Supremacie.

Yf commaundement were giuen to Cities and tounes Corporate that they should speciallie regard to those Such officers as were wise, godlie and favorers of the truthe.

Yf Justice and iudgement were severelie without respect of person executed, and vice and Sinne in all Sortes of people sharplie punished.

Yf the ministers of goddes word were all compelled to consent in one truth and preache one doctrine, faithfullie and prudentlie with all diligencie to do their office and to liue in good order.

Then I wold not doubt but god should haue his glorie, this realme should florishe, the prince liue in greate comfort, and the people in good order and much quietnes. Thus praing the all mightie god to graunt you the Spirite of wisedome, that you may governe to his glorie, the honor of the prince and to the good of the Commenwealthe, I Commend your honors to his gratious direction and merciefull tuition.

Ffrom my house at Hartilburie, this xxvii[th] daie of october 1564
  Your honors humble at Comandement,
  E. S. WIGORN.[a]

[a] Edwin Sandys.

f. 2a.

[The first column contains a list of "Gentillmen of anie worshipp or name now abiding in Worcestershire;" these are then classified as below. To avoid repetition the names of the residences which it supplies have been added to the classified list. The only names not classified are those of Richard Hobbie of Elmsleie Castell, gent.; Anthonie Wollmore of Kington, gent.; and John Hall of Hallowe, gent. The note is added that John Talbot, Esquier, and Gilbert Talbot, Junior, are now not resiant within the shire.

The second column contains a list of the "Justices of peace resiant within Worcestershire." To avoid repetition, the information this column supplies is added to col. 4. It then continues:]

Col. 2.

Hedde officers and other rulers temporall within the countie of Wigorn:

Sir Edward Saunders, knight, Lord chief baron, iustice of assise; Thomas Carus, esq., Sergiant at Lawe, Justice of Assise; William Sheldon, esq., custos rotulorum; Sir Thomas Baskervile, knight, High Sherif; Sir Robert Throckmorton, knight, Highe Steward of the landes of the dissolvid monasterie of the abbaie of Evesham; Sir Robert Throckmorton, knight, Highe Steward of the landes of the bushopp of Wigorn.

Sir John Bourne, knight, high Steward of the landes of the House of Wigorn; Sir Thomas Russell, knight, Surveior of the landes of the bushop of Wigorn; William Conniers, esq., Surveiur of the quenes majesties landes with in the countie of Wigorn; John Wallwen, gent., Surveior of the landes of the house of Wigorn; William Cookeseie, esq., vndersteward of the landes of the dissolvid monasterie of Evesham; Clement Swalow, gent., vndersteward of the landes of the bushop of Wigorn; Thomas Cecill, gent., vndersteward of the landes of the house of Wigorn; Edmund Colles the quenes maiesties Excheater for Worcestershire; John Hornicold, esq., Auditor aswel of certen of the quenes landes as also of the busshoppes whole Landes.

[Col. 3 contains a list of Coroners, whose names will be found below; of " Hedde officers within the Citie of Wigorn," whose names will be found below except that of John Throckmorton, esquire, recorder; a note that " The bailiffes and aldermen are allwaies Justices of the peace with in the Citie by their Corporacion ; of Hedde officers for the ecclesiasticall politie, whose names and offices are entered below;" and a note that " Bailiffes of small corporate Townes are here omitted because they are removeable everie yeare."

Col. 4.

Favorers of true religion :

Edwinus episcopus ; Sir Thomas Russell, knight, of Strensham, Justice of peace resiant within Worcestershire ; Sir Thomas Pakington, knight, of Hampton ; William Ligon, esq., of Madresfield ; John Littelton, esq., of Frankleie ; Thomas Blount, esq., of Kitterminster ; Robert Hunckes, esq., of Blockleie; Miles Sandes, esq., of Fladburie ; Anthonie Daston, esq., of Bradwaie ; William Jeffreis, esq., of Homme Castell ; Richard Smith, esq., of Upton on Severn ; Frauncis Welsh, esq., of Shellesleie Welsh ; Anthonie Washburn, esq., of Wichenford ; John pakington, esq., of Chaddesleie ; Thomas Horton, esq., of Staunton ; Edmund Harewel, gent., of Besford ; Gilbert Littleton, gent., of Claines ; Roger Littleton, gent., of Groveleie ; William Rouse, gent., of Aberton ; Robert Gower, gent., of Witleie ;   Kettilbie, gent., of Codderidge ; Thomas Barnabie, gent., of Bockleton ; Bartholomewe Hales, gent., of Fladburie ; William Harrison, Coroner, of Parshor; Thomas Doding, bailif, of Wigorn ; Richard Bullingham, alderman there ; John peddar, deane of the Cathedral Church ; Thomas powell, Chauncelor and Archdeacon.

Nota.

Adversaries of true religion :

Sir Thomas Baskervile, knight, of Birlingham (High Sheriff) ; Sir John bourne, knight, of Holt;[a] Henry Dingleie, esq., of

[a] Signs as J. P. to Act of Uniformity, 1569. On his enmity to Sandys, see *State Papers*, p. 223.

Cropthorne; John Knottesford, esq., of Greate Malvern, William Cookeseie, esq., of Stulton, Justices of peace resiant within Worcestershire; Michaell Ligon, esq., of Powike; William Conniers, esq., of Belbroughton; John middemore, gent., of Kingesnorton; William Sparrie, gent., of Kingesnorton; William Heath, gent., of Allchurch; Robert Blount, gent., of Asteleie; Thomas Lewkener, gent., of Allchurch;   Lench, gent., of Dardall; Jeffreie Markham, esq., of Feckenham; Arthur Wood, gent., of Claines; Thomas Bourne, gent., of St. Johns; Connand Richardson, gent., of Parshor; William Moore, gent., of Powike;   Morgan, gent., of Hanbury; Richard Badland, (Bailiffe in the citie of Wigorn); John Concher,[a] alderman (in the Citie of Wigorn); Thomas Cecill; Thomas p(o)pe of Malvern, Coroner; Edward Darnell, (Town clerk); William Warmesbreie, Register.

Col. 5.

Indifferent in religion or else of no religion:

William Sheldon, Esq., of Beoleie (Custos Rotulorum), John ffolliot, esq., of Pirton, Edmund Colles, esq., of Lighe, John Rouse, esq., of Rouselench, Justices of peace resiant within Worcestershire; William Gower, senior, esq., of Woddall; Charles Acton, esq., of Elmeleie Lovet; Walter Blount, esq., of Sillington; John Hornicold, esq., of Blakmore park; Frauncis Braze, esq., of Dardoll; John Abington, esq., of Hallowe; William Nunfand, gent., of Berrowe; Nicholas Clifton, gent., of Clifton; William Gower, Junior, gent., of Boulton; William Gower, gent., of Witleie; Richard Barnabie, gent., of Acton; Henry field, gent., of Kinges Norton, Coroner; William Child, Clerik of the peace; Thomas Cotterell, of Erlescrome, Coroner.

Men fit to be Justices of the peace in the countie of Wigorn:

Episcopus; Sir Thomas Russell, knight; Sir Thomas pakington, knight; William Ligon, esquier; John Littelton, esq.;

[a] Signs Act of Uniformity, 1569

William Sheldon, esq.; Thomas Blount, esq.; Robert Hunckes, esq.; Miles Sandes, esq.; John ffolliot, esq.; Edmund Colles, esq.; Anthonie Daston, esq.; Richard Smith, esq.; John Rouse, esq.; William Jeffreis, esq., mort.*; Frauncis Welsh, esq.; John Abington, esq.; Edmund Harewell, gent.; John Peddar, deane; Thomas Powel, chauncelor.

Men fit to be Shiriffes :
Sir Thomas Russell, knight; Sir Thomas Pakington, knight; William Ligon, Esq.; John Littleton, esq.; William Sheldon, esq.; Robert Hunckes, esq.; Thomas Blount, esq.; John ffolliot, esq.; Anthonie Daston, esq.; Frauncis Welsh, esq.

[Col. 6 contains a list of " Justices of peace in that part of Warwickshire which is within the dioceses of Wigorn," whose names are classified below ; of " Hedde officers and other rulers within that part of Warwickshire"—Sir James Diar, knight, Justice of Assise ; Sergiant Benlose, Justice of Assise, & the High Sheriff & the Queen's Receiver (see below) ; & of " Hedd officers in the ton of Warwick," whose names, except that of John Ditch, are classified below as Governors.]

Col. 7.
Ffavorers of true religion :
John ffisher, esq., high shirif; Thomas Lucie, esq., of Charlecote, Clement Throkmorton, esq., of Haseleie, Justices of peace in that part of Warwickshire ; Robert gibbes, esquier, of Honington; Giles Palmer, gent., of Barton on the heath ; William Huddesdon, gent., of Warwick, Governor ; James Langwurth, gent., of Tisoo; Charles Ramesford, gent., of Wotton Worwen.

Aduersaries of true religion :
Sir Robert Throkmorton, knigh(t), of Coughton, Justice of peace in that part of Warwikshire; Sir William Wigston, knight,

* Note in Burleigh's hand. " William Jeffreis " is scratched out.

recorder; John Somerfield, esq., of Eddenston; Frauncis Smith, esq., of Wotton Worwen; Edward ferrys, esq., of Cock Levington; Thomas fisher, esq., of Warwik, the quenes receaver; Thomas Vnderhill, esq., of Etington; John Vnderhill, esq., of Grimstoke; Thomas Knottesford, gent., of Studleie; Hedgock, gent., of Salford; John Comes, gent., of Stratford; Graunt, gent., of Snitterfield; William Skinner, gent., of Rowington; Clement Swalow, gent.; Richard Roo, bailif.

Richard ffisher, John ffisher, Thomas Barrett, William Edmundes, Richard Townesend, Roger Edgeworth,* town clerk, Gove(rnors).

Indifferent in religi(on) (or) of no religion :

Sir John Conwaie, knight of Arrowe; fouke grivell, esq., of Beauchamp Court; Thomas Throkmorton, esq., Justice of Peace in that part of Warwickshire; Anthonie Trussell, esq., of Billesleie; Anthonie Ingram, esq , of Litle Wolford; Thomas Rowleie, gent., of Utlecote; Richard Middlemore, gent., of Studleie; Richard Hall, gent., of Utlecote.

John Butler, Thomas Oken, John Nason, William Hill, governers.

Robert Gibbes is a fit man to be a J(ustice) of peace.

Endorsed : To the quenes Maiestie most honorable Privie Counsell.

f. 5.

My dutie humbly considered. Vnderstandinge by your honorable lettres the Quenes maiesties most earnest intention for thadvauncement of true religion to represse obstinate adversaries, as I greatly reioyce, so haue I employed my endevour (as shortnes of tyme would suffer) to satisfie your lordshippes commandement requiringe spead. Ffirst, thankes be to almightie god, through the Quenes most gracious government, assisted by your lordships providente circumspections this Countye of Sussex whereof, as an humble

* Written Sogworth in col. 6.

servitour, I execute the ecclesiasticall Jurisdiction, is fre from all violent attemptes eyther to afflite the godlye or to distourbe the stablisshed good orders of this Realme. Notwithstandinge I doubte of secrett practises which perhappes myght breake oute into open violence, were yt not for feare of your Lordshippes vigilante Aucthorite. It is to be wished that men of honour, whyles they be resiante in the sheire, to haue learned preachers of their own or others, shewinge themselves wyllinge to heare the worde of god, whose example draweth a nombre of people after them. Concerninge the matter I haue vsed conference with Mr. Dean of Sarum and Mr. Augustine Bradbridge, my Chancelour, bothe of them borne in the shire and thoroughly acquainted with the state of the same. I refrayned to communicate so franckly with others because I doubted of there secretnes, that retinue and alliance beinge so great in theis partes. Also the chefest to be trusted nighe vnto me at this pointe were from home. Thus commendinge your honours to the tuition of our saviour christe,

Ffrom Allingborne the xxvii[tie] of this Octobre,

Humblie at Commandment,

W. Crestren.[a]

f. 7.

The countye of Sussex very narrowe in breadeth is about lx myles in Length and is devided into two partes East and West.

Col. 1.

In the west parte:

Justices of peace which be favourers of religion and godlye orders:

Sir Thomas Palmer of gadwode, knight, A fainte furtherer;[b] Mr. Henry Goringe of Westburton; Mr. Jhon Apleye of Thacham, learned in the lawe;[b] Mr. Henrye mervin of Rogate; Mr. William Bartlett of Stopham.

[a] William Barlow, Bishop of Chichester.　　[b] Notes in another ink.

Justices of peace which be myslykers of religion and godlye procedinges:

Mr. William Shelley of michelgrove; Mr. William Dautrey of moore, Verye supersticious;[a] Mr. Edmonde Forde of Chartinge, Extremely perverse;[a]

Gentlemen being no Justices favourers of godlie procedinges:

Mr. Jhon ffennour of Amberley; Mr. William Stanney of the manwoode; Mr. Richard Crulie of Cackham.

Gentlemen beinge no Justices myslykers of godlie orders:

Mr. Richard Lewknour of Ttrotton; Mr. Thomas Stoughton of Stansted, a stoute scorner of godlines;[a] Mr. Thomas Lewknour of Tangmer; Mr. William Devenishe of Chichester; Mr. William Stapleton of Ovinge, wickedly obstinate;[a] Mr. Arthure Gunter of Rackton.

Col. 2.

In the East parte:

Justices of peace which be favourers of Religion and godlie order:

Mr. George Goringe of Ovingdean, learned in the lawe; Mr. Jeferye of Chittinglye,[b] learned in the lawe;[a] Mr. Jhon Hussey of Cukfilde; Mr. Richard Elderton of Wiston; Mr. John Limmesford of Easthothly.

Justices of peace which be myslykers of religion and godly procedinges:

Sir Edward Gage of fferle; Mr. Jhon Thatcher of Westham; Mr. Richard Coverte of Slowham;[b] Mr. William Culpeper of Ardinglie; Mr. Henry Poole of Dechelinge; Mr. Edward Bellingham of Newtymber; Mr. Thomas Parker of Wyllington; Mr. Thomas Dorrell of Stackney; Mr.   Robertes.

Gentlemen being no Justices favourers of godly procedinges:

Mr. Anthony Pelham of   ; Mr. Jhon Pelham of

[a] Notes in another ink.
[b] Signed the Act of Uniformity, 1569. D.S.P. lx. 22.

Lawghton;[a] Mr. Jhon Selwyn of ffriston; Mr. Laurence Ashburneham of Gestlinge; Mr. William Morleye of Glyne; Mr. Anthony Stapley of ffranfeld; Mr. ffrances Spilman of Hartfeld.

Gentlemen beinge no Justices myslikers of godlie orders:

Mr. James Gage of Broyle, A common herborer of obstinates;[b] Mr. Shelley of Patchinge; Mr. Drewe Barrentyn of Horstid kaynes; Mr.   Scott of Edon.

On the back (f. 6a), Col. 1.

The tounes in the west parte:

Laurence Andreu, maior, Rafe Chantelor, Steward, notorious obstinate aduersaries.[b]

Thomas Addams, Thomas Palmer, Jhon Moyses, Jhon Cooke, Thomas ffaringdon, frowardly supersticious.[b]

Of whom the last three be Justices of the peace within there Liberties by a late Commission which were better for gover(n)mente of the poore Citie to be revoked and the Cittizens to be as they were before vnder som order of the Justices at Large.

Col. 2, parallel column.

The tounes of the east parte:

Rye, Hastinge, Lewes, and Brighthelmeston ar governed with suche officers as be faythfull favourers of goddes worde and earnestly given to mainteyn godly orders.

Endorsed f. 8 b.: To the right honorable Lordes of the Quenes majesties privie counsell.

f. 9a.

My dewtei most humbly vnto your honors remembred. These ar to aduertise the same that I receaved your most honorable letters the 20 of october dated at S. James the 17 of the same monthe: which according to my bounden dewtey I haue with all diligence considered and altho I am persuaded that to certefie your honors according to your commaundment maie procure me moare hatered (which neadeth not) and what as hatered can do, yet my

[a] A J. P. Oct., 1569.   [b] Notes in another ink.

dewte of obedience to your honors, the advauncement of goddes honor and the comfort of good and faithfull subiectes (which your honors will me herein to respecte) hathe for the present driven awaie fearfulnes of offending any person. So that I haue frely, planely and also truly (so far as either myne owne skill and knowlege or the skill and knowlege of others whome in this matter I haue vsed can reache) certefied your honors to euery point of your said letters.

ffor this certeficat (because my chauncelor doeth ordenarely ride abought my diocese vi or vii tymes yeareley and therfor like to haue good knowlege of gent(lemen) in the same) I vsed his counsell and advise. In like manner I vsed the deane of the cathedrall church of Hereford and singularly euery deane rurall for his owne deanery wherin he ys deane, which do best knowe the gent(lemen) in their severall deaneris and thus thorowe their skill and myne owne, I haue certefied as foloweth; most humbly beseching your honors to take in good parte owr simple & plaine dealing and by your discrete and godly wisedomes so to use and order both us and this good cause that we be not brought hereby in to further hatered, contempt or daunger than must neades folowe.

Your honors to commaund
Jo. HEREF.[a]

The names of soche persons as now beare rule in the countei of Hereford and diocese of the same which be demed not favorably to this religion :

John skudamor [b] of Home, esq., one of the counsell of the Marshes of Wales iustice of peace. Custos rotulorum. Hie stuard of vrching fie(l)d and stuard of the cytye of Hereford.

Richard Seborne of Sutton, esq., on of the said cowncell & iustice of peace ; John skudamor of Kenchurch,[c] esq., iustice of peace ;

[a] John Scory.
[b] Signed the Act of Uniformity, 1569. D. S. P. lx. 22.
[c] Refused to sign.

Thomas Havard of Hereford, esq., iustice of peace; Thomas Clynton of Estenor, esq., iustice of peace ; John Huband abbots Hybottes [a] of Hampton, esq., iustice of peace ; Richard Harford of bosbery, esq., no iustice, but the Quenes majesties generall surveior (as I haue learned) of all Hereford shere, and receivor to her majestei of Soche landes as belonged lately to the bishop of Hereford ; John Clarke of Hereford, gent., no iustice, but he ys clarke of the peace and exerciseth the office vnder Mr. liggen of bishopes castell in Shropshire which favoreth not this religion.

John James of Stretton ; John Crouse of brobery, no iustices, but thei be the crowners for the county of Hereford.

f. 9b.

The names of soche persons as now beare rule in the cowntei of Hereford and diocese of the same which be demed newters in religion.

Sir James baskervile,[b] knight of   , iustice of peace; John Harley[b] of bramton, esq., iustice of peace and rular of Wigmores land ; Symon Apparry[b] of   , esq., iustice of peace ; george Apparry[b] of paston. Hie Shrefe of the countei of Hereford the yeare now past and ended ; Richard monington of Sarnisfeld, iustice of peace ; gregory price of Hereford, esq., iustice of peace.

The names of soche as now beare rule in the countei of Hereford and diocese of the same which be iuged favourable to this religion.

John [b] bushop of Hereford on of the counsell of the marshes & iustice of peace.

Sir James Acroft, knight, of croft, iustice of peace, Sir Robert Whitney of Whitney, knight, iustice of peace; Hughe Apparry[b] of Aconbury, esq., iustice of peace ; Walter Vauhan of brodwardene, esq., iustice of peace.

[a] Called below John Hibotes of Hampton.   [b] Signed in 1569

James Warmecombe [a] of Wington, iustice of peace; John Patsall of the forde, esq., iustice of peace; James boyle of Hereford, esq., iustice of peace. These iii be learned in lawes of the realme.

John Abrall of Eustane, esq., iustice of peace.

The names of soche as be now no iusticeis in the countei of Hereford which, for the favoure which thei beare to this religion and of good giftes, are mete to be called to be iusticeis.

John Ellys,[a] deane of the cathedrall churche of Hereford, a divine.

Edward threlkeld of ledbery, doctor of the lawes and chauncelar of the dyocese of Hereford; Edmond Horwell of Cradley, esq. This gentleman (because part of his house standeth in Worcestershere notwithstanding bothe his bedchamber and parishe churche called cradley aforesaid ar in Hereford shere) accounteth himselfe of & with that shere of Worceter & neverthe(less) because ther be moare in Worcetershire that favore this religion than be in Herefordshere, your honors shuld do very well to command him to serue the Quenes maiestie in Herefordshere.

Nicholas Debden of ludford, esq.; John Heward of ledbery, gent.; John myntrige of cradley, gent.; John garnans of Hereford, gent., meanely learned in the lawes of (the) realme; Thomas Kirll of Walford, gent., learned in the lawes of the realme.

f. 10a.

The citei of Hereford ys fraunchesed and ys governed by a Mayer whome the comens do yearely chose of the common cowncell or election.

The names of the common counsell or election which be demed no favorers to this religion.

Thomas Havard, iustice of peace, which by common fame ys a daily dronkard, a receivar & mayntainar of the nnemeys of religion, a mayntener of supersticion and namely of abrogated holydaies.

[a] Signed in 1569.

He vseth to praie vpon a laten primer full of supersticions. His
wife & maydens vse bedes and to be short he is a mortall ennemy
to Christen religion (thus doeth Mr. Deane of hereford write vnto
me, which I partly knowe and partly beleave to be true.)

Rowland rice; Harry Dodson; Walter caredyne; Thomas
churche;[a] William raulyins; Richard partriche,[a] Senior; Richard
partriche, Junior; William runell; James Eiton; John Clarke,
toune clarke; John Darnell; Richard bromwich; John Seward;
Father Chalice; Mathewe geffres; John Clyotes, an atturney at
the lawe; John Hyde; John partriche of bothale; Humfre
Wilbram; William benet.

The names of soche of the said councell or election that be iuged
neuters in religion:

John gibbes;[a] John maylar,[a] mayer for this yeare; Thomas boyle;
Richard vele; Harry grene; John pearle; Thomas russell; Thomas
currant; John Whitlache; Edward Welche.

So that of the holl counsall or election ther is not on that ys
counted favourable to this religion.

f. 10b.

The names of soche persons as nowe beare rule in the countei of
Salope that dwell in or veri neare the diocese of Hereford which be
demed not favorable to this religion.

William gatacre of clarely, esq., iustice of peace; Adam Watley
of pitsford, esq., iustice of peace; Richard amytton of Salope, esq.,
iustice of peace; Thomas eyton of eiton, esq., iustice of peace; John
farmor, dwelling in Briggenorth parke, esq., iustice of the peace.

The names of soche persons as now beare rule in the countei of
Salope and dwell in the diocese of Hereford which be counted
newters in religion :

Sir george blunt, knight of Kenlet, Hie shrefe of shropshire this

[a] Signed in 1569.

last yeare now almost ended; Charles Soye of bromfild, esq., Secretory to the counsell of the marshes and iustice of peace; Richard Cornewall of burford, esq., iustice of peace.

The names of soche persons as now beare reule in the countie of Salope which be demed favorable to this religion and dwell in Hereford diocese:

Harry lord Stafford of Cawas iustice of peace; Edward leighton of Wattesborowe, esq., iustice of peace; Symon Kemsei of ponsbery, esq., iustice of peace; Thomas Willyams of Wollaston, esq., iustice of peace. This gent maye also serue in mungommery shere because he dwell very neare that s(here).

The names of soche as be favorers of this religion in the countei of Salope and dwell in the diocese of Hereford not yet in office, neuertheless thought mete to be called to be iustices:

Richard lawley of Wenlocke, esq.; Thomas lodlowe of the morehouse, esq., baily of Wenlock; William leighton of plashe, esq., learned in the lawes of the realme; Rowland lacon of Willey, esq.; Lewes Jones of bushopes castell, esq.; John Hopton of Morcaild, esq.; Fraunceis Cresset of Staunton lacey, gent.; Edmond Cornewall of burford, gent.; Edward Hopton of bitterley, gent.; Adam lutley of bromscroft, gent.

f. 11a.

Radnor:

The tounes of old radnor, new radnor and prestene be in the diocese of Hereford and veri litle moare of that cowntei ys in the said diocese, whereas none of the iustices of peace that be now in office ar cownted favorers of this religion but the best of them ys iuged but a newter.

Ther names be:

John bradshawe theldar of prestene, esq., iustice of peace; John bedo of prestene, iustice of peace; Perse lloyd of prestene, iustice of peace; Roberd Vauhan of prestene, iustice of peace, but counted a poore man; Edward pre of Kington, esq., iustice of peace; Thomas lewes of old radnor, iustice of peace.

The names of soche as favoure this religion in the countei of radnor, and dwell in the diocese of Hereford, which ar now no iusticeis but yet meete to be called thervnto :

John blayney of Stepleton in the parish of prestene, gent.; John madockes of barlanton in the parish of old radnor, esq.; Edward threlkeld of ledbery, doctor of the lawes and chauncelar of Hereford (because he rideth ordenarely vi. or vii. tymes yearely in to that part of radnorshere that ys in Hereford diocese as well as in to others, might serve well ther in the place of a iustice of peace considering ther ys so litle choise of soche as be favorable to this religion.

Worcetorshere :

Certeine villages also of Worcetershere be in the diocese of Hereford, whearas be iii. gentlemen, The first ys John throgmorten of ribbisford, esq., on of the councell of the marshes and iusticeis ther, demed not favorable to this religion. The second ys William geffres of Homme Castell, esq., now iustice of peace and iuged to favoure this religion. The iii^{de} ys fraunces Welshe of litle shelsey, esq., accounted a favorer of this religion, no iustice now but mete to be called thervnto.

monmoth :

The toune of monmoth ys in the diocese of Hereford and no moare of that countey, and ys gouerned by a mayer which ys yearely chosen by the commens of the toune and ii balies.

The names of soche as be not counted favorable to this religion in the toune of monmoth :

More Appowell, recorder of the towne.

CAMD. SOC.   D

William G[ui]ll[i]m, Thomas Williams of the priory, Roberd Williams, his sonne, of the common counsell.

The names of soche as be demed favorable to this religion in the toune of monmoth :
William bunting, mayer this year.
Huegh baker, Edward Ag[ui]ll[i]m, balies this year.
John knight, Crownar, John Waters, clarke of the peace, James leighton, gent., meanely learned in the lawes of this realme.

f. 12a.
Hereford :
The toune of lempster in the countei & diocese of Hereford ys fraunchesed and gouerned by a baley yearely elected.
George Monons [a] balei this yeare a simple man and a neuter in religion demed.

The favoreres of religion in the said toune as counted to be these folowing :
Fraunces Philips, gent.; John Hingeley, gent. ; John strete ; Thomas Dallow, gent. ;[b] Richard stede ; John poil, baker.
I can not heare of any enneineis to this religion in the said towne that be of any reputacion.

Salope :
The towne of lodlowe yn the countei of salope & diocese of Hereford ys also a fraunchesed towne, whear the counsell of the marshes do commonly lie.

The names of soche as ar demed to favoure this religion in the said towne ar these :
Laurence Beck, Richard raskall,[c] bailies this yeare.

[a] Monox. G. F. Townsend, p. 293.   [b] Bailiff, Townsend, p. 293.
[c] Mirror for Men of Ludlow, p. 107. Ric. Baskoll, 1596, was put into the new corporation made by Elizabeth, with William Beck, Richard Blashfield, and — Walker.

Simon thornton, Scolemaster; Nicholas Debden of lodford, esq., he dwellith hard by the said towne; Richard Walter, gent., learned in the lawes of the realme; Thomas Blasfeld, gent.
The rest of this towne are cownted either ennemeys or newters.

Hereford:
Ther be also in this diocese and countey of Hereford diuerse fostered and mayntayned that be iuged & estemed some of them to be learned, which in Quene Marys daies had livinges and officeis in the churche, which be mortall and deadly ennemys to this religion. Their names be blaxton, mugge, Arden, Ely, frier gregory, Howard, Rastall of gloceter, Jonson, menevar, Oswald, Hamerson, ledbery and certeyne others whose names I knowe not. These go from on gentlemans house to another, whear thei know to be welcome which (as S. Paule writeth of some soche like to titus) *totas domus subuertunt, docentes quae non oportet, turpis lucri gratia.*[a]

The cheafe and principall receivors & mayntencrs of these ar William luson, canon residensari of Hereford, the vecars of the quere ther, Thomas Havard of Hereford, iustice of peace. John skudamor of Kenchurche, iustice of peace; John Hibottes of Hampton, iustice of peace; Richard Harford of bosbery, esq.; Thomas Croft of Ocley, esq.; William berington of Winsley, esq.; Thomas Clynton of Estnor, iustice of peace; Thomas berington of cowarne, gent; James eiton, William Russell, John Ely & John Hide citezens of Hereford and of the common counsell ther.

And of these ther be certeine thought to haue masseis in their houseis, which come very seldome or not at all to churche, which neuer received the communion since the Quenes majesties raigne openly in the church, which keape as it wer scoles in their houses of popery, deriding and mocking this religion & the ministers

[a] Titus i. 11.

therof, which be a marvelous stombling block to the Quenes
majestes loving subiectes in this countei. Seing in them and som
tyme also hearing of them, soche contempt of religion without
correction or controlment as for my part I remember the wise saing
of iesus the sonne of Syrac, *iudex evadere ne contendas, ne inique
factis par esse non possis.*[a] I must neades confesse that I am not
able to reforme these, except I shuld be mightely backed by your
honorable auctorite, and haue those worshipfull iusticeis which ar
demed favorers of religion to be more ernestly ayding than thei
haue ben; to enterprise a matter; and not able to finishe the same
accordingly, shuld encrease furthe derision, contempt and hatered
with out profit. Therfor I referre this to your most honorable
consideracion and godly wisdom.

f. 13a.
Hereford:
Further whearas your honors willed me by your said honorable
letters that I shuld also aduertise the same yf ther war any other
thing within the said diocese of hereford that might tende to the
redresse of the disorder you wrote of, (which you meane to remedei)
Maye yt please your honors to be advertesed that yf the cathedrall
churche of Hereford war reformed, the citei also and the countei of
hereford, yea, the holl dyocese, wold sone be by goddes grace be (*sic*)
in like maner reformed. Besides myne owne knowlege Mr. John
Ellys, deane of the said churche, hathe certefied me as foloweth :
thet all the canons resedensaries (except Jones, *qui dicit, et non
facit* which ys rashe, hastei and ondiscrete), ar but discemblers and
rancke papistes. And these haue the rule of the churche, and of
all the ministres and officers of the same, and ar neither subiect to
the ordenary iurisdictyon, neither of the deane, nor of the bushop,
but war reserued inmediately to the vsurped iurisdiction of the
bishop of rome, and nowe to the Quenes majestei (as thei saie)
which thei clayme and hold by prescription. So that now thei

[a] Eccl. vii. 6. Ed. Tigurina.

maie do what thei list without controlment. Thei neither obserue the Quenes majestes iniunctions given vnto them in her highnes visitacion, nor the archebusshope of Cantorberis iniunctions given them in his visitacion, nor yet the iniunctyons of the Quenes maiestes hie commissioners (wherof I send herein vnto your honors a copei). The communion was not ministred in the cathedrall churche since ester (as I am enformed). The canons will neither preache, reade homelis nor minister the holy communion, nor do any other thing to commend, beautefie or set forwardes this religion, but mutter agenst yt, receive and mayntaine the ennemys of religion. So that this churche which shuld be the light of all the diocese ys very darkenes, and an ensample of contempt of true religion, whome the citei and countre abought folowe apase.

The said deane hathe also certefied me that the vecars of the Quere, the deacons and sextons be all mortall ennemys to this religion, receivears and mayntenars of soche as themselves be.

S. Paule compareth false doctrine and religion to the kanker called *gangrena* which (except yt be quickly cured & healed) neuer ceaseth creping and infecting on part & member after another, tyll yt hath distroied the holl bodey.

Your honors by your wisdome can consider howe daungerous and perlous vnto the holl ecclesiasticall and politicall body of this dyocese this fretting and creping canker ys, when yt doth once possesse the heade churche of all the diocese. The only remedy wherof ys, that yt maie please the Quenes majestei to committe either an ordinary iurisdiction or soche auctorite as shall please her highnes, to whome yt shall please her majestei, that maie and will vrge them either to do as becommeth good christean subiectes and faithfull ministers or els to place others in their rom ther that will do accordingly.

f. 13b.

Die veneris xx die februarii a° dñi 1561 pa[d] lambeth coram Rev[mo] patre Matheo Cantuar archiepiscopo ac Rev[do] patre Edmundo London episcopo et Roberto Weston legum doctore commissioniariis regiis.

Hereford :

An order for Mr. William luson prebendary of Hereford and others the prebendaries ther, enyonyed vnto them by the said commissioners to be executed and red inmediatly after the reading of the homelys every daie in their order and corse.

Good people, yt ys very requisite that some publike testification be made that the ministers of the church consent and agre in on vnite of doctrine and religion, by reason wherof yt ys very well ordered in this churche agreable to the Quenes maiestes iniunctyons that the principall ministers of the same shuld so do by preching, reading of homelys and other declaration, that no scruple shuld remayne in the myndes of the people of any difference or dissentyon to be emongst vs, and therfor for my part do willingly testefei my assent to the godly publike reformacions established by the lawes of this realme and namely in these two artikells folowing:—

Ffirst I am in conscience persuaded that the churche of england ys a true member of the holy catholike churche. And that the Quenes maiestei ys by right and iuste title the supreme gouernor of the same churche of England next and inmediatly vnder our saveor iesus christ, bothe in matters ecclesiasticall and temporall; and that neither the bushop of rome nor any other foreine powre, potentate or prelate hathe or ought to haue any maner auctorite or iurisdictyon in or over the said churche of England.

I am also persuaded and do confesse that the order of administracion of sacramentes, the common praires and other rytes and ceremoneis prescribed by the boke of common praire ar sincere, true and good, and consonant to the doctrine of holy scriptures, and the auncient vsage of the holy catholike churche of christ.

Item, that the said Mr. luson shall minister the communion in the cathedrall churche of hereford on some sondaie or holy daie after thende of ester weake next comming.

Item, that he shall reade the homely of salvacion on that daie or some other sondaie in the said cathedrall churche before the first daie of maye next comming, so that on of the Canons of the said churche, being no prechar, doo reade on before him, and all other canons of the said churche being no prechars to do the like in their turnes, on soche daies as ther shall be no sermon.

Concordat cum registro, William bedell.

f. 14a.

Yf your honors wold cause these formar iniunctions to be put in execution, yf the canons themselues wold not receive any good therby, yet I trust that the people shuld, or at lest this good must neades come hereof, that thei shuld discredite themselues, yf thei shuld in secret speake ayenst that which thei had confessed openly in ther churche: because I cold not get any of the canons that dwell in Hereford to reade the first homely according to the formar order, I sent in to shropshere to on Parson Normcrote,[a] a canon of that church of Hereford, to come and reade an homely according to the said order: who did yt, and that very well: whervpon I thought that Mr. luson & the rest wold have folowed but thei did not, nor never will except thei be forced by auctorite & cetera.

Endorsed: To the moste honorable the Quenes maiestes privei cownsell my veraie good lordes.

f. 15a.

Blessed be the almighty and everlasting god, in whose handes ar the hartes of all kynges and princes, who hath moved the harte of our most gratiouse Soverayne, and the hartes of her maiestes most honorable cownsell, to consyder in tyme the state of goddes true religion, daungerously declyning in the most partes of the churches in this realme. Our heavenly father who hath moved her maiestes harte and yours also graunt your Maiesti and you all her honorable cownsell, as godly courage as god wisshed and gave to Moses, Josue, David and opers his godly gouernours, to thintent this realme may be blessed, and goddys holy name glorified, *et vos reportetis immarcessibilem gloriae coronam.*[b] Now for answere to

[a] Roger Normecote, collated 23 March, 1560-1. Le Neve, i. 505.
[b] 1. Peter v. 4.

your honours letter. Towching the Justices in Cambridge shyre, I haue conferred with Mr. Chicheley, Mr. Hutton, Mr. Hynde and Mr. Pygot. Towching the Justices of the Isle of Ely, I haue conferred with Mr. Hopkins, Mr. Dixon and Mr. Adam. Towching the Justices for Cambridge, I haue conferred with Dr. Hawforde, Dr. Ithel, Dr. Stokes, Dr. Kelke, & William Mownsey now Maior, and in Cambridge it is most requisite to have Justices of good religion. And as I can learne, there ar iii sortes of Justices concerning godly religion, sum good, whom I haue noted with this letter "g." Sum conformable, whom I haue noted with this letter "c." Sum mislyked, apon whom I haue sett no signe. And because your honours do requyre me to signifie whom I thinke most mete for service that way, who commonly serue in the quorum, I have enterprised to note my fansye with this letter "q" apon their heads, who ar thought metest. And further because your pleasure is, that if I consyder of any other thing, tending to your godly meaning for the redresse of this disorder, I shulde signifie the same to your honours, I have noted my poore opinion in a by papyr, to be expended of your wisdoms. And thus I trust I haue answered your honours expectation after my rude maner. Ffor my parte I will after my poore witt and vnderstanding travaile according to your most godly meaning, and call apon god with my harty prayers, alwayes to assiste you in this most nedeful busynes. The lorde Jesus prosper all your godly affayers. Ffrom Ely the vith of Nouember, 1564.

Youre honours to commaunde,
Richarde Ely.[a]

f. 16.

Commissioners for the peace with in the countye of Cambrydge:

q. c. Edwarde Lord Northe of Kellynge; *q. c.* Sir Gyles Alyngton of Horshed; Sir Robert Chester of Royston; *q. g.* Sir Roger Northe; Sir John Coton of Landnad ; *q. c.* Barnet Ffrevell of Shelforde ;

[a] Cox.

q. c. Mr. Robert Payton of Isleam; *g.* Mr. Frauncys Hynde of Madingley; *g.* Mr. Henrye Pygot of Abyngton ; *q. g.* Mr. John Hutton of Drydrayton; *c.* Mr. Jhon Myllecent of Berham ;[a] Mr. Thomas Homes of Barrogrene; *q. g.* Mr. Chycheley not in commission.

Commissioners for the peace in the Isle of Elye:
q. g. Mr. Antonye Stapleton cheffe iustyce hear.

Commissioners resiant with in the Isle :
g. Mr. Gefferey Colvill of Newton ; *q. g.* Mr. Robert Balam of Wysbiche; *g.* Mr. Edwarde stewarde of Chatteresse ; *g.* Mr. Thomas Wren of Hadnam ; *q. g.* Willyam Adam of Tyd ; *g.* Mr. William Bryan of Leueryngton; *q. g.* Mr. William Hopkyns of Elye; *g.* Mr. Raffe Dyxon of Duddyngton.

Commissioners of peace not resiant in the Isle:
g. Mr. ffrauncys Hynde; *c.* Mr. Robert Payton ; *g.* Mr. Henrye Reppys; *c.* Mr. Rycharde Payton ; *g.* Mr. William Thorneton ; *g.* William Adam of Ely, mete to be in commission ; *q. g.* Dr. Ithell chauncelar to the Bysshope.

Commissioners for the peace in Cambrydge :
The vycechauncelar and the mayor for the tyme beynge.
Jhon Porye [b] Dr. of Diuinitye ; *c.* Henrye Hervey,[b] D. of Lawe ; Alexander Raye, Alderman; *g.* Robert Shutt, recorder;[c] Phylyp baker, D. of Dyuynytye; *q. g.* Thomas Ventris, Alderman ; *c.* Henrye Searle,[d] Alderman ; *g.* Roger Slegge,[d] Alderman.

[a] All these signed the Act of Uniformity, 1569.
[b] Signed the Act of Uniformity.
[c] M.P. 1571. See Cooper's *Annals.*
[d] Enquiries on their conduct in *State Papers,* Addenda, 1564, No. 29, p. 553. See too *State Papers,* September 14 and October 24, 1564.

Men mete for the commission there :
q. g. Dr. Hawforde, Master of Christes college ; *q. g.* Dr. Bewmant, Master of Trynytye college; *q. g.* W. Mounsey nowe maior ; *g.* Dr. Stokes, Master of Quenes College. The multitude of Justices thought not nedefull.

Endorsed : To the Quenes Maiestes most honorable cownsell.

f. 18a.

My dewtie first accordinglie remembered to your honours. Hit may please the same to be aduertisedd that for the accomplisshinge of your pleasures vttered vnto me in the lettres, which I receaved the xxth daye of October last paste, I haue conferred with certen archdecons Comissaries ande Officialls excreisinge iurisdiction within the precincte of my office whom I know to be men bothe learned and honeste, and likewise to have good knowledge bothe of them that are in auctoritie and in commission for the peace at this present in the place where they exercise iurisdiction ande also of others, beinge owte of commission, who in their opinions are meete to be called ᵃ therevnto. The effecte ensuinge of that owre conference your honours shall perceaue by the shedells or papers herevnto annexed. In the which allso I haue written certen articles, which in my opinion may serue for remedies of certen disorders, levinge the same to your godly consideracions ande commendinge yowr honors to the blessed gouermente of all myghtie godd. Ffrom Bugden this viith of November 1564.

Your honours to commaunde

f. 20a. N. LINCOLN.ᵇ

Lincoln:

Justices of pece there :

Richard Dismy, armiger, Edmund Hall, armiger, Robert Carr, esquier, Anthonie Harrold, earnest in religion.

Roberte Dymocke, esquier, Roberte Harringtonne, mort,ᶜ esquier, William Tharrold, esquier, hinderers.

ᵃ A word illegible. ᵇ Nicholas Bullingham.
ᶜ Note in Burleigh's hand.

Kesteven:
Richard Bartie, esquier, Thomas Saintpoll, esquier, John Aelmer, archdeacon of lincoln, Thomas Godwine, canon residenciarie of lincoln, William Porter, esquier, Charles Wynfeld, gent, Richard Meares, armiger, James Harrington, gent., Earnest in relligion and to be trusted there.

Justices of peace there :
Adland Welbie, esquier,   Hunston, esquier, Johnne Manne, gent., earnest in relligion.
Leonard Irbie, gent.,   Holland, esquier,   Ogle, gent., indifferent.

Holland :
Richard Bartie, esquier, Thomas Saintpoll, esquier, John Aelmer, Archdecon of lincoln, Thomas Godwine, canon residenciary of lincoln, Edmundd Lyall, esquier, William Derbie, esquier, Laurence Meares, esquier, Earnest in relligion and to be trusted there.

f. 20b.
Justices of peace :
Sir Richard Thimelbie, knyght, Sir William Skipwith, knight, Thomas Saintpoll, esquier, Roberte Mounson, esquier, Laurence Meares, esquier, Adland Welbie, esquier, Earnest in relligion.
Sir Edward Dymocke, knight, Richard Bolles, esquier, Charles Willoughbie, esquier, Cristofer Wraw,[a] esquier, James Smyth, esquier, Tristrame Tirwhite, esquier, William Manbie, esquier, Antonie Tomeney,[b] esquier, Richard Craicroft, esquier, Indifferent.
Sir Roberte Tirwhite, knight, Johnne Copledicke, esquier, Humfrey Litlebury, esquier, hinderers.
Richard Bartie, esquier, John Aelmer, Archdeacon of Lincoln, Thomas Godwine, canon residenciary of lincoln, Thomas Morrisonne, gent., earnest in religion and fitt to be trusted there.

[a] ? Wraye, in S. P., ii. 17.   [b] ? Tourney, in S. P., ii. 17.

f. 21a.
Countie of the citie of Lincoln:
Aldermen there :
Iohn Hutchinson, Maior, Nicholas Ffawkoner, earnest in relligion.

Thomas Wright, George Stampe, William Goodknap, William Kent,[a] George Porter,[b]   Ffulbecke,[c] Leon Ellys,[d] indifferent.

Richard Carter,[e] William Scolfeld,[f] Edward Hallelary,[g] hinderers.

Martine Hollingwourth, late alderman, veray earnest in relligion, honest and pollitique.

The names of them with whom I haue conferredd :
Mr. Jhon Aelmar, archedecon of lincoln, Mr. Thomas Taylor, regester, Mr. Thomas Sainctepoll, esquyer.

f. 21b.
The Corporacion of Grauntham, Comburgisies (*sic*):
Roger Jonsonne, Thomas Tilson,[h] John Tailor, earnest in relligion.

Simon Hanson, Gabriel Best, John Picke, Thomas Sympson, Robert Gibbon, indifferent.

Humfrey Duckar, alderman, George Atkinson, Roberte Wright, John Brotherton, Edward Mortonne, hinderers.

f. 22a.
Bedfordshere:
All Justices now in commission:
Lewes Mordent,[i] esquyer, Lewes Dyve,[i] esquier, Thomas pygott, esquier, John Thomson,[i] esquier, Thomas Leigh,[i] esquier, Robert Nedegate,[i] esquier, Earnest in religion.

Humfrey Ratliff,[i] knight, Peter Gray,[i] esquier, Raulf Astrye,[i] esquier, indifferent.

John Gascoyne,[i] knight, John Cowlbeck,[i] esquier, John Ffuller,[i] esquier, hinderers.

[a] Mayor 1572. See Lincoln, names of Mayors, &c. [b] Mayor 1575.
[c] Mayor 1565.   [d] Mayor 1572.   [e] Mayor 1577.
[f] Mayor 1576.   [g] Mayor 1567.
[h] Robert Gibbon scratched out.
[i] All in Pat. Roll., 6 Eliz., pt. 3, mem. 1.

Henry Cheney, knight, Reynold Grey, esquier, John Burgoyne, esquier, John Swifte, esquier, Thomas Snager, esquier, Henry Ackworth, gent., earnest in religion and fytt to be trusted.

The Corporacion of Bedford. Out of Comission:
Thomas Leigh esquier, Thomas Dyve gent., Earnest in religion.
Rycherd Laurence, William Bull, hinderers.
Henry Laurence, Alexander Hunt, Earnest in religion and fytt to be trusted.

The names of them with whom I have conferred:
Maister Addams, minister, Maister leighe, esquyer.

f. 22b.
Huntingdonshyre:
All Justices now in Comission:
Robert Tyrwhit, knight, Rychard Darington, esquier, earnest in religion.
Laurence Tallard, knight, William Laurence, esquier, Gylbert Smithe, esquier, Robert Fforest, esquier, indifferent in religion.
Thomas Cotton, esquier, a hinderer of religion.

Oute of Comission:
Henry[a] Cromwell, knight, William Mallary, esquier, Thomas Worlege, gent., Robert Awdeley, gent., earnest in religion and fytt to be trusted.

Thauncient of the corporacion of Huntingdon:
William Symcotes, gent., Thomas Harrys, Robert Blyncthorne, John Turpen, earnest in religion.
Henry Dackham, gent., William Wallys, William Bushe, John Rychardes, hinderers in religion.
Charles Rigges, Rychard Mayre, Anthony Dixon, indifferent in religion.

[a] Henry scratched out.

I haue conferred with maister William Slaed, comyssary for this shere.

f. 23a.

Hertfordshere:

Justices and now in comission:

John Brockett, esquier, George Horsey, esquier, Thomas Dockwray esq., Rowland Lutton, esq., Nycholas Bristow, esq., earnest in religion.

John Butler, knight, John Twyneo, esquier, Mr. Burgoyne, esq., Mr. Purvey, esquyer, hinderers of religion.

Oute of Comission:

Mr. Tucke, esquier, John Nedam, esq., earnest in religion & fyt to be trusted.

I haue conferred for this shere with Mr. William Slayd, comissarie and Maister smythe, minister.

f. 24a.

Leicestershire :

All Justices nowe in commission :

Sir Thomas Nevell of Holt, knight, George Hastinges, esquier, Adriane Stookes de Barrowe, esquier, Ffrancisce Cave de Baggrave, esquier, Briane Cave de Ingersbie, esquier, George Turpyn de Knaptoft, esquier, Nicholas Beamount de Coloverton, esquier,

Brokesbie de Sholbie, esquier, Leonard Dannett de dannet hall, esquier, Ffrancisce Broune de Kilbie, esquier, earnest in religion.

Mighell Purefey, esquier, George Vincent de peckleton, esquier, Smyth de dalbie parva, esquier, indifferent.

William Skevington de Skevington armiger, hinderer ; Maurice Bartley de Womendham, esquier, indifferent ; Laurence Saunders, gent., hinderer.

Mr. Outreade de Burton lazars, esquier, learned and wise, William Blounte de Osbaston, gent., Thomas Roose de Lutterwourth, gent., Thomas Ashebie de Losebie, gent., Thomas Brahm de Barrowe, gent., John Nowell de Willesborough, gent., Temple de ead[em], gent., earnest in relligion and fitt to be trusted.

f. 24b.

The Corporacion of Leicestre. Annceantes of the Corporacion there :
William Manbie, Johnne Hericke,[a] Richard Davie,[b] Darker,[c] Inglish,[d] Clarke,[e] Gillott [f] senior, earnest in religion.
Halame,[g] Raignoldes,[h] Stamford,[i] Tatham,[j] indifferent Nix, Maior,[k] Ffletcher, Ffowler,[l] Morice,[m] hinderers.

The names of them with whom I haue conferred :
Maister John Aelmer, Maister Thomas Larke, comissary and officall.

f. 26a.

Buckinghamshyre :
Justices and now in comission :
Paule Darrell, esquier,[n] Thomas Pygott, esquier,[o] Thomas Fflitwood, esq.,[p] John Cheney of Amersham,[q] Mr. Cade of Dorney, John Doyley, esquier, Willelmus Day, prepositus Eton, Thomas Tyrringham, esq.
William Garrett, knight, Edmund Ashfield, esquier,[r] John Goodwyn, esquier,[s] Nicholas West, esquier,[t] William Hawtree, esquier,[u] Richard Hamden, esquier, indifferent in religion.
Robert Drurye, knight,[v] Edmund Wyndzore, esq., John Cheney of Chessham boyes,[w] hinderers of religion.

[a] J. Thompson, Leicester, p. 251, gives him as Mayor, 1572.
[b] Ib., 1563, 1575.   [c] Ib., 1560.   [d] Ib., 1570.
[e] Ib., 1569.   [f] Ib., 1571.   [g] Ib., 1561, 1574.
[h] Ib., 1562.   [i] Ib., 1573.   [j] Ib., 1567, 1577.
[k] Ib., 1564.   [l] Ib., 1565.   [m] ? Noryce, ib., 1579.
[n] Lipscombe, I. xvii., High Sheriff, 1562.   [o] Ib., 1570.
[p] Ib., 1563.   [q] Ib., 1567.   [r] High Sheriff, 1568.
[s] Ib., 1561.   [t] Signed the Act of Uniformity.
[u] High Sheriff, 1558 ; signed the Act.
[v] High Sheriff, 1560 ; signed the Act.   [w] High Sheriff, 1565.

32 LETTERS FROM THE BISHOPS

Oute of Comission :
Henry Lee, knight, Thomas Packington, knight, Robert Stafford, knight, William Fflitwood of the temple, Robert Mordant, gent., Rychard Craiford, gent., Roger Alford, gent.,[a] John Purefrey, gent., John Burlacye, gent.,[b] Wiliam Shepherd, gent., Mr. Croke of Chilton, gent.,[c] Paule Wentford, gent., earnest in religion &' fitt to be trusted.

f 25b.
Thomas Pigott, esquier,[d] Mr. Tyrill, esquier, Rychard Hichcok, gent., Alexander Denton, gent., Mr. Harcote of lechamstede, William Cornewalle, gent., William Biseley, gent., Thomas Rede, gent., Thomas Wayneman, gent., William Clarke, gent., Robert Newdegate, gent., Walter Wynzore, esq., William Wyndzore, esquier, Mr. Pymme, Baron of thexchecour, Rychard Payne, esquier, indifferent in religion.
Robert Peckham, knight,[e] William Dormer, knight,[f] Robert Pygott, gent., Thomas Gifford, esq., Mr. Hamdon of Hartwell, Mr. Scrope of Hambledon, Davy Pen, gent., John Newdegate, gent., George Hansley, George Peckham, gent.,[g] Edward Ardes, gent., Rychard Ffarmer, gent., Ralf Haydon, gent., Mr. Rookes of Ffawley, hinderers of religion.

These bee they with whom I did conferre :
John Longland, Archdeacon of Buckingham, John Cheney, esquier, Mr. Ffyssher, preacher.

f. 27a.
Remedies for disorders :
1. A comission to be graunted to certen chosen persons bothe of the Clergie and laitie to extende as well to places exempte as not

[a] Signed the Act. " Mr." is corrected to " Roger."   [b] Signed the Act.
[c] High Sheriff, 1574.   [d] High Sheriff, 1570.
[e] Died at Rome, IV., 451.   [f] High Sheriff, 1567.
[g] High Sheriff, 1572.

exempte, within liberties and withoute, for reformacions of disorders in religion.

2. That the said comissioners haue auctoritie to reform all suche papisticall orders and vsages in cathedrall and collegiat cherches as by theire discrecion shall appeere woorthie reformacion.

3. Som conuenyente order to be taken with the romisshe sectuaries, as well beinge in durance as straglinge abrode, for reformacion of theire obstinacie which dothe mvtche harm amongste the people of god and the queen her maiestes subiectes.

4. The iustices of peas to be charged to be present at everie quarter sessions where they shall cawse the articles, accorded vpon for vniformitie in religion, to be openly redd and then to be confyrmed and allowed of by theire severall actes in subscribinge openly to the same.

5. That thenqueste then to be panyelled may be charged to certifie in theire veredictes all suche whom they shall learn to maynteyn any contrarie opinion, and that the forsaid comissioners may haue auctoritie to reforme suche offendours accordinglie.

6. That the archedecon comissarie and officiall or the woorthiest of them may be in the commission of peas with in the circute of his office and that the same haue in charge to be presente at everie quarter sessions, where on of them or som other learned man vpon theire appointement, shall make a sermon concerninge the setting forthe of the doctrin conteyned in the said articles.

f. 27b.

To everie cathedrall cherche the dean and residensaries shall by coarse make everie of them ones in a quarter a sermonde. And in the same, after the prayers, shall read openly and distinctly the said articles of religion allowinge then of the same by his open confession and shall allure others therevnto.

> Endorsed: To the moste honorable lordes of the queen her maiestes priuie cowncell.

CAMD. SOC. F

f. 30.
Certayne brefe notes of your honors to be considered :[a]

1. Ffirst the learned aduersaries being ecclesiasticall persons to be ether banished or sequestred from conference with such as be fawtors of there religion, or elles the othe to be tendred vnto them. Forthwith, considering thei haue so litle passed of the Quenes maiesties clemencye, to them shewed these six yeares, whereby it doth appeare that they be more stubburne & more incoraged than thei ware before.

2. Item, that the stragling doctors & priestes who haue libertie to stray at there pleasures within this realme do much hurte secrettlye and in corners, therefore it weare good that thei might be called before the highe commissioners and to shew there conformitie in religion by subscrybing or open recantacion or elles to be restrayned from there said libertie.

3. Item, a proclamation to be sett forth by the quenes maiesties aucthoritie, to represse the bold talk and bragges of the aduersaries of good religion, and by the same proclamation that the ministers of goddes word might be incoraged to vse there function without feare, who be now in a manner nothing estemed.

4. Item, a commission to be awarded as the highe commissioners haue at London at this present, whearein the bysshopp of the diocesse and other lerned men & good gentellmen might haue aucthoritie bothe to inquyre and reforme the aduersaries of good religion and to represse the fawtors of the same.

5. Item, whereas Regesters for the most parte haue there office by patent being corrupt in religion, who do more hurte knowing the state of the diocesse and being in greate estimacion with the aduersaries of good religion then the prechers are able to do good otherwayes, therefore it weare mete that the bysshopp might haue aucthoritie to remove them owt of there roomes allowing them a certayne resonable stypend and to place theim that did favor the setting forth of good religion.

[a] This appears to be from the Bishop of Peterborough, Edmund Scambler.

6. Item, whereas the chefe Constables of euerye hundred which be ringe leders of the people and whom the people haue in greate credytt and for the most parte be fawtors of naughtie religion, that it might be provyded that the commissioners by the consent of the the bysshopp, vppon iust occasion might haue aucthoritie to remove them and to place other in there places.

7. Item, there be diuerse gentellmen of euell religion that kepe scholemasters in there houses privatelye, who be of corrupt iudgementes and do exceding greate hurte as well in those houses where thei teaches as in the Countrie abrode abought them, that it might be provyded that the sayd gentellmen should not kepe privatelye in there houses no maner of scholemasters but ssuch as should be examined by the bysshop of the diocesse and admitted thereunto by licence vnder his seale of office.

f. 30b.

8. Item, that the Prebendaries of euerye Cathedrall churche maye be inforced by aucthoritie to make a manifest and open declaration of there faithe before the congregacion by thappoyntment of the Bysshopp of the diocesse, and in there said declaracion to sett forthe the aucthoritie of this religion by parliament established and by goddes word confirmed, and that thei do openly professe and geve there consent to the same, detesting all other religion to the contrarye, and also shall subscrybe to the articles of Religion agreed vppon in the presence of the Bysshopp and other commissioners appoynted for the reformacion of religion.

f. 31b.

Comitatus Northamton :

Nowe in the commission of the peace :

Sir Walter Myldmaye, knight, Sir Roberte Lawe, knight, Mr. Edwarde Mountague, esquyer, Edmonde Elmes, esquier, George lynne, Mr. Moungomerye, Mr. Wattes, esquiers, earnest furtherers of religion.

Mr. Ffrauncys Saunders, esquyer, Thomas Spencer, esquyer, indifferent in religion.

Nowe in the commission of the peace :
Mr. Valentyne Knightley, Sir John Spencer, Sir Thomas Gryffyn, Sir John Ffarmer, knightes, Edwarde gryffyn, Mr. Catesbye of Whyshyn, Thomas Lovett, esquiers, greate letters of religion.

And now owt of the commission of the peace :
Edmounde Brudenell, John Wake, esquiers, John ffosbrooke, Bartholomew Tate, Jhon Pyckeryng, Mr. Coope of cannonsashbye, John Dreyden,[a] James Crewes,[b] Roberte Pemberton, gentellmen, Mr. Anthonye Burton, bachelor of diuinitie and chancellor of Peterboroughe, earnest furtherers of religion and worthie to be trusted.

f. 32a.
Burgh Socon being a peculiar libertie :
Esquiers and now in the commission of the peace of that libertie.
Roberte Wyngfelde thelder, Fraunceys Quarles, Roberte Wyngfelde the younger, Roberte Browne, earnest furtherers of Religion.
Jhon Mounstwing, gentellman, a greate letter of religion, and now in commission for the peace within the same libertie.
Peter Kemppe, gentellman, an earnest furtherer of Religion within the same libertie, and now owt of the commission of the peace.

The Corporacion of Northampton :
Mr. Bawgye, Mr. Cole, earnest furtherers of religion and now in the commission of the peace within the same towne.

[a] Jhon Wake, scratched out.   [b] Wake corrected to Crewes.

Conitatus (sic) Rutland :
James Harrington esquyer, earnest furtherer of religion and now in the commission of the peace there.

Mr. Dyckbye of Stoke, indifferent in religion.

Mr. Anthony Collye, Mr. John Hunt, Mr. Calcott, esquyers, greate hynderers of religion and now in commission of the peace there.

Mr. Anthonye Burton, Bachelir of divinitie and Chancellor of Peterburgh, Mr. Mackworth, Mr. Jhon Harrington of Exton, Mr. Fflowre of Whytwell, earnest furtherers of religion there & worthy to be trusted, and now owt of the commission of the peace there.

f. 34a.

Right honorable, after my most humble commendations, it maye please your honors to understand, that upon your honours letters lately directed unto me, I have considered of the Justices for the peace wythin the counties of Wiltshyre, and Barkshire, whiche counties bothe lye wythin the dioces committed to my charge, and in seueral schedles haue noted owt bothe theire names and dwellinge places, and also theire sundrie inclinations towardes the furtherance of Goddes truethe, and that sincerely, and uprightly, and wythout al partialitie, accordinge to the trust that your honours haue reposed in me toutchinge the same; wherin also I haue used thaduise of sutche gentlemen as in the seueral schedles unto your honours maye appeare. Thus I humbly take my leaue and wyshe unto your honours the sprite of wysedome, and thencrease of Goddes grace.

From my poore house in Sarum, 9 Nouemb. 1564.

Your honours most humble
Jo. Sarum.[a]

[a] Jewell.

f. 35a.

The names of the Justices for the peace wythin Wiltshire :
John Meruin of Fountel, knight, No hinderer ; John Thinne of Longleate, knight, A furtherer earnest; John Zouche of Ansty, knight, A furtherer earnest ; George penruddock of Iuychurche, A furtherer earnest ; Nicolas Snel of Kington S. Michaelis, No hinderer; Edward Baynton of Rowdon, No hinderer ; Edward Baynard of Lakeham, A furtherer earnest ; Henry Sharington of Lacocke, A furtherer earnest ; Richard Kingesmyl of Ouerton, A furtherer earn(est); Jo. Sainctjohn of Lidiard, No hinderer; Jo. Byre of Chalfyld, No hinderer ; Christofer Willugbee of Litle Knoel, No hinderer ; Christofer Dodington of Meere, A furtherer ; Jo. Berwike of Wilcote, No hinderer; Jo. Hooper of Sarum, No hinderer ; Giles Thistlethwaite of Winterslowe, A furtherer ; Henry Boddinham of Fulstone, No hinderer.

Other gentlemen of your honours to be consydered :
George Ludlowe, a furtherer, Laurence Hyde, a furtherer, Henry Clyfford, a furtherer, Al wyse and politique and hable to serue.
Wyth thaduise of Sir Jo. Zouche.

f. 36a.

The names of Justices for the peace wythin the Countie of Berkshyre :
Henry Neuil of Ruscombe, knight, A furtherer earnest; Richard Warde of Hurste, as it ys supposed no hinderer ; Thomas Welden of Cookham, A furtherer; Thomas Stafford of Bradfild, A furtherer; John Winchcombe of Bucklebury, A furtherer ; Edmund plowden of Shiplake, as it ys supposed a hinderer ; Jo. Cheyney of Woodhay, A furtherer; Griffith Curteis of Greenham, A furtherer earnest; Roger Yonge of Bustyldeane, A furtherer earnest ; William [a]

---

[a] Cor. from Jo.

Dunche of Litle Wittenham, A furtherer earnest ; Jo. Fetiplace of Beselslygh, A furtherer; Robert Kelaway of Shallingford, A furtherer; William Hyde of Denchworthe, No furtherer.

Jo. Yate of Buckland, neuer yet received the holy Communion sythence the beginninge of the quenes maiesties reigne, and therefor nowe excommunicate, and returned into the kinges bench for the same.

One gentleman of your honours to be consydered :
Edmund Dokwra, of Chamberhouse,[a] a furtherer and learned.

Wythe thaduise of John Winchecombe and Griffith Curteis.

> Endorsed : To the right honorable and my singular good Lordes, the Lordes of the queenes maiesties most honorable privy councel.

f. 38a.

Right honorable & my very good lordes, with all humblenes these may be to signify vnto you, that having receaved the xxvi[th] day of October last, your honores letteres, bearing date the xvii[th] day of the same monethe, according to my bounden duety, with all speed and diligence that I cold vse in suche diepnes of waies, and distance of the persones from me with whom I might confer, I have endevoured my self taccomplishe your commaundement, and answer your expectation in certifying of suche Justices of the peace as ar communly resiaunt within the severall shyres of my Dioces or Jurisdiction. Wherin for my better procieding, I first vsed the counsell of Mr. Nowell, Dean of Lichfield & James Weston, my Register, men godly & zelous, of longer continuance, and therby of more knolege and experience in my Dioces than I ; by whose advyse I sent for suche persones as were thoght most miet, for love

_a Inserted.

to Justice & zeal for religion, to confer with for suche effect as in your honoures letteres is specified, and so vsing & folowing their advise to that end, I have first simply made certificate after the same, adding consequently that opinion which I have of them severally conceived, by commun reporte of suche credible men as I have to do with in my dioces, and myn oun daily experience: Partly that your honores may vnderstand the opinion of those with whom I have conferred, and partly what I here & vnderstand of them by commun reporte of good men otherwys. And wheras your honoures moved me to advertise you of any other thinges tending to the redres of disorderes within my dioces, ffor the county of Stafford where my habitation is, by meanes wherof I have better vnderstanding of the commun doinges then in other places, thies few thinges I have to signify, vnder your honores correction.

ffirst, for the county of Stafford bicaus ther be not many learned men in the same, it is thoght a great hinderance to Justice, that they which be lerned & Justices, ar also commun counselleres in the shyr, by which meanes ether the Quenes maiestie is not faithfully served or the clientes not iustly helped; of thies I here diverse complain.

Secondly, the number of attorneis, frequenting the assizes and sessiones at Stafford, are iuged to bried and norishe matters of stryf & contention betwien party & party for their lucre sake: which if it might be otherwys helped, is thoght good to many men.

Thirdly, wheras the cuntry is to miche hinderly in all good thinges perteining to religion, yet the abyding of Doctor Poole, late bishop of Peterboro, in that shyr with Bryan ffowler, esquier, a litle from Stafford, causeth many pieple think wurs of the regiment & religion then els they wold doo, bicaus that diverse lewd priestes have resort thither: but what conferens they have, I can not learn. Wherfor if it pleas your honores to remove him from thens, you shall doo miche good to the cuntry, and frustrate thexpectation of evill disposed persones.

ffourthly, I have bien moved diverse tymes by many godly men, to labour vnto the Quenes maiestie or to your honores for a commission, wherby I might better do my deuty, for that many offenderes ar ether born with by M[aster]ship, which I alone can not redres, or els fly into exempt places & peculiar Jurisdictiones and so avoid ordinary correction, not without great offence and slaunder bothe of the gospell & ministeres therof, which thing I refer to your godly wisdom to consider as occasion shall move you.

f. 38b.

Last of all, the greatest disorder within my hool Dioces, hathe bien in great tounes corporate; for there when I have required thassistaunce of the bailiffes or other officeres, I have found open resistance in matteres of charge, wherof it is niedfull to place good men in office there; & yet presently I am not able to make certificate who be best affected in those tounes, for that many of them ar visited with the plage. And therfore thies may be to desyr your good honores to take this certificate in good parte, even so committing the same to the mighty & mercifull protection of almighty God, who kiep you all in long, peacefull and helthfull lyf.

this x^{th} of November 1564, at Eccleshall Castle.

Your good honores with all humblenes and obedience to command

THOMAS COVEN. & LICH.[a]

f. 40a.

An Information or Certificate made to the Quiens maiesties most honorable privy Counsell by Thomas, Bishop of Coventry & Lichfield of all the Justices of peace resiaunt within the severall shyres of his Dioces, and of suche persones as ar miet to be called to the said office as folowethe. Novembris, 10, $a°$ 1564.

[a] Bentham.

Of Stafford shyr, after thadvice of Thomas Wirley, John Lane & Roger ffoulk, esquieres.

The Lord Viscount Hereford of Chearkley, The Lord Stafford of Stafford Castell, The Lord Dudley of Womburn, Sir William Snede of Broodwall, knight, Sir George Blunt of Knightley, knight, Sir Raffe Bagnall of Delacres, knight, Humfrey Wells of Horecros, esquier, Raffe Okover of Okover, esquier, Thomas Wirley of Hamstede, esquier, Edmund James of Corbenes, esquier, John Leveson of Wolverhampton, esquier, Rafe Adderley of the Holt, esquier, Bryan ffowler of the Manor of Sowe, esquier, miet to continue in office.

Sir Edward Aston of Tixall, knight, Sir William Greisley of Colton, knight, Simon Harecourt of Ranton, esquier, a knot hurtfull to Justice & great Mainteineres.

Henry Vernon of Hilton, esquier, an adversary of relligion.

Sir Edward Litleton of Piliknoll, knight, Sir Raffe Egerton of Wreinhill, knight, John Rottesley of Rottesley, esquier, John Lane of Hyde, esquier, Roger ffoulke of Gonstone, esquier, miet to be called to the office.

f. 40b.

The Bishopes advise & opinion for the Justices of Staffordshyr as foloweth.

Althogh by thopinion of those men whose advyse I vsed for Stafford shyr, dyversmen be thoght miet to continue in office, of whom I hear litle commendacion otherwys, Thies may signify vnto your honoures that by the common report of many men godly & credible & by that knowlege & vnderstanding that I have, thies persones folowing, viz. :—

Sir William Snede, knight, Sir George Blount, knight, Humfrey Wels, esquier, John Leveson, esquier, Rafe Adderley, esquier, Bryan ffowler, esquier, ar accounted of good men adversaries to religion & no favoureres therof, nether in died nor woorde.

Concerning the hurtfull knot & Henry Vernon esquier, I nied

say no more. Ffor I looke that that which is by otheres confessed wilbe laid to my charge, if you stand not my good Lordes.

As touching suche persones as ar thoght miet to be called to the office, I have nothing to say to the contrary bicaus I hear well of them all.

The best learned in the county of Stafford.

Thomas Wirley of Hamsted, Edmund James of Corbenes, Roger ffoulk of Gunstone, no Justice as yet, favoureres of Relligion & Lerned.

Humfrey Wells of Horecros, Rafe Adderley of the Holt, Bryan Ffowler of the manor of Sowe, no favoureres of Religion but better learned than the rest.

f. 41a.

Of Darbyshyr, after thadvyse of Sir Thomas Kockein Knight, Waltar Horton, esquier, & Aden Berisford, esquier, as foloweth :—

Sir John Zouche [a] of Codner castle, knight, Sir William Sentlow of Chattesworth, knight, Sir George Vernon of nether Haddon, knight, Sir Ffrauncis Leke[a] of Sutton, knight, Sir Thomas Cockein[a] of Ashburn, knight, Godfrey ffuliambe[a] of Walton, esquier, Thomas Stanhope[b] of Aibley, esquier, Thomas Sutton of Over Haddon, esquier, James Hardwik[b] of Hardwik, esquier, Antony Gell of Hopton, esquier, miet to continew in office.

Sir Humfrey Bradborn[c] of Lee, knight, Henry Vernon of Sudbery, esquier, adversaries to religion.

Richard Blakwall[d] of Calk, a lawier, Godfrey Boswell[e] of Beighton, esquier, miet to be omitted.

Walter Horton of Catton, esquier, George Curson of Croxall, esquier, Thomas Kniveton[f] of Mirkaston, esquier, Richard Wenslow of Wenslow, esquier, Aden Berisford of Bently, esquier, Rafe

[a] Signed for the supremacy.   [b] Absent at the signing.
[c] Sheriff, 1563, 1574. Other sheriffs were Zouche, Leke, Cockein, Ffuliambe, Stanhope.
[d] Not a Justice, 1569.   [e] Signed the supremacy, 1569.
[f] A Justice, 1569.

Sacheverell of Staunton or Radburn, good men & miet to be called to office.

f. 41b.

The bishopes advyse concerning the Justices of Darbyshyr.

Concerning the certificate made before, I judge all very well done, according to my knolege and vnderstanding save only in two persones viz :—

Sir George Vernon,[a] knight, is knowen to be a great Jester at Religion as well as in all other thinges.

Also I have a good opinion of Mr. Blakwall, a man of good learning with whom I have diverse tymes talked & so do lyke well of him and think him miet to continew in office.

And as touching those which are thoght miet to be called to the office, they all have a good reporte bothe for civill Justice and favour to religion as any men that I know or hear of.

Anthony Gell[b] of Hopton, esquier, is accounted learned.

f 42a.

Of the countie of Salop, after thadvyse of Sir Andrew Corbet knight, Sir Richard Newport, knight, and George leigh, Bailiff of Salop, as foloweth :

In diocesem Coventry etc. :

Justice Corbet of Stoake super Tern, Sir Andrew Corbet[c] of Mourton Corbet, knight, Sir Richard Newport[c] of Arcoll Magna, knight, Sir Arthur Manwayring[c] of Hightfield, knight, Richard Corbet of Painton,[c] esquier, Georg Bramley of Worfield, esquier, James Barker of Haghmond, esquier, Adam Otley[c] of Pitchford, esquier, Thomas Scriven[c] of ffrodisley, esquier, Humfrey Onslow of Salop, miet to continew in office.

Extra diocesem Coventry :

Edward Leighton[c] of Wattelsboro, esquier, Simon Kensey of the

[a] Not a Justice, 1569.   [b] Signed the supremacy, 1569.
[c] Signed the Act of Uniformity.

Okes, esquier, Thomas Powell [a] of Whittington, esquier, Lewis Johnes [a] of Bishopes castell, esquier, Charles ffox of Bramhill, esquier, Richard Cornwall [a] of Burford, esquier, miet to continew in office.

William Charlton of Wombridge, esquier, William Yong of Kainton, esquier, Thomas Eton of Eton, esquier, William Gatacre [a] of Gatacre, esquier, adversaries of religion.

Robert Corbet of Stannerton, esquier, Robert Neidham of Shenton, esquier, John Hourd of Bridgnorth esquier, George Leigh of the toun of Salop, bailif, William Gratewood of Adderley, esquier, Rafe Cliff of Wayvart, esquier, Peter Banister of Hadnall, esquier, Miet to be called to office.

f. 42b.

The bishopes advyse for the countie of Salop :

Concerning the certificate before made of the Justices of the county of Salop I iudge it to be well done, so that I can nether iustly chaunge, add or take any thing away, for that knolege which I have : and yet I do know well all the persons save only those which be extra diocesem Coventry, etc.

I know the learning of none muche reported, but of Justice Corbet, and George Bramley.

As touching the toun of Salop :

Humfrey Onslow, esquier, Edward Hosier, esquier, George Leigh, now bailif, Robert Ireland thelder, Robart Ireland the yonger, aldermen & counselleres of the toun miet to bear office, bicaus many tymes corrupt men ar chosen to be bailifes.

Thomas Aston, Scholemaster, and a worthy man emongst them. Ffor Bridgnorth :

John Hourd esquier, a wyse and godly man.

Of Warwikshyr after thadvyse of Edward Eglamby esquier.

Sir Richard Verney of Compton Verney, knight, Thomas Lucie

[a] Signed the Act of Uniformity.

of Chalcot, esquier, Basill Ffielding of Munkes kirby, esquier, Clement Throckmorton of Haselye, esquier, Simon Arden of Warden, esquier, John ffisher of Packington, esquier, Edward Eglamby of Meryden, esquier, Henry Godyer of Polesworth, esquier, Good men & miet to continew in office.

Sir William Wigson of Woolston, knight, William Devereulx of Meryvall, esquier, Simon Rawleighe of Ffarmboro, esquier, John Hibalt of Ipsley, esquier, John Middlemore of Edgebaston, esquier, Thomas Lysley of Moxall, esquier, indifferent persones.

Sir Robert Throckmorton of Conghton,[a] knight, Thomas Throckmorton of Morehall, esquier, Michael Purefey of Calcat, esquier, no favoureres of religion.

The bishopes opinion touching the certificate made of the Justices of the county of Warwik.

Fforasmiche as myn abyding is far of frome that parte of my Dioces, and partely through good Justices of peace, & partly by the diligence of myn Archdeacon Mr. Leaver, & other Rurall Deanes, I have bien litle trobled with any matters, by meanes wherof I have not travilled so miche that way to get any vnderstanding by myn own experience. I do here confes to your honores that I iudge this former certificate made good and sufficient for that shyr. Adding this, that I wrote & sent for mo of that shyr to confer with, namely for Clement Throckmorton, esquier & Henry Goodyere, esquier, who presently be at London, or els the certificate had bene witnessed with mo.

Now if it may stand with your honores pleasure to consider of suche a commission as in my letteres is mencioned with humble (f 43b) peticion, and think the same miet to be graunted. Then thies may signify vnto you with lyke humblenes, the names of certain Ecclesiasticall persones whom I do think & iudge miet for that purpose to be Joyned with suche of the reste as your wisedomes may appoint, being noted ether as miet to continue or to be called vnto office, within this former certificate, viz. :

[a] Corrected from Morehall.

Laurencius Nowell, Decanus Lichfield; Robertus Weston, Cancellarius Episcopi; Thomas Levir, Archidiaconus Coventry; Thomas Bickley, Theologiæ Baccalaureus; Arthurus Bedle, Legum Baccalaureus; Thomas Ashton, Clericus, Ludimaderator (*sic*) Salop; Robertus Aston, Rector de Muccleston; Petrus Morwing, Rector de Langforde; Augustinus Bernhear, Rector de Southam.

Thomas Coven. & Lich.

f. 44b.

A certificate of the Justices within the Dioces of Coventry & Lichfield.

> Endorsed: To the right honorable and his very good lordes of the Quienes maiesties Privy Counsell thies be given.

f. 45a.

Suffolk.

My humble dutie vnto your honours remembred, pleaseth it the same to be advertised that having receved your honorable lettres to certefie such Justices and hed officers of the Shire of Suffolk as be eyther favorers or myslikers of the orders of this Realme established for thecclesiasticall pollicye of the same, and that I shold do the same by thadvice of such men of gravitie and knolege as I shall thinke mete for that purpose to enforme me for the vnderstonding therof, having the rule and authoritie eyther as Justices of peax or other hed officers within my Jurisdiction, being not favorable to the ordinary good procedinges of this Realme, in the orders and cawses of Religion, and likewise who they be that be well geven and mete to continew in office, with their names and dwelling places, as I haue donne for the shire of Norffolk as may farther appere to your honours by my certificat of the same,[a] and meaning to do the like for Suffolk where, perceving ther ys some discention as well for religion as otherwise, least the mallice of the one part or

---

[a] Below f. 58.

the other might be occasion for me to certifie more than truthe, and yet not meaning to omitt my dutie, I haue thought good to vse thonlie advice of myne officers there, by whom I vnderstond that thes persons vnderwritten are not so well bent vnto the advauncement of the godlie procedinges of this Realme in cawses ecclesiasticall as other the Justices of that Shire be : viz. : Sir Clement Higham and Sir John Tyrrell,[a] knightes. Mr. Tulmach of Helmingham, Mr. Robert Gosnall of Otley, Mr. John Sowthwell of Bartham, Mr. Ffoster of Copdock, Mr. Payne of Burie, Mr. Barbour, baylif of ypsewich, and yet I must testefie as in my certificat of Norffolk that I nether know or yet can lerne probablie of anie fact, that eyther Sir Clement Higham or Mr. Gosnoll are to be charged withall, but for the rest I dare not testifie so farr, being not by common fame accompted of such zeale and good affection toward the religion now established as ys necessarilie required in men of their authoritie and calling, the displacing or reformacion of which I must holie committ to your honorable consideracions, as one having little accesse thither or acquaintance among them. And so leving farther to troble your honours I commend the same to the protection of Almightie god. Ffrom Norwich this xixth of November 1564.

   Your honours humble to commaund

            JOHN NORWIC.[b]

f. 46a.

In most humble manner certifiethe vnto your honours that accordinge to your letters to me directed and dated the xviith of October I have hadd conference with suche grave, wyttye men, good in Relligion as favourers of the policie of the Realme nowe

---

[a] *State Papers,* vol. 60, No. 62, iv. Among those who have been of the Commission and presently be not.
[b] Parkhurst.

established, namelye Mr. Alane Bellingham, Mr. George Lampleughe, Mr. Henry Towson, Mr. Richard Dudley, Mr. George Scroope, sub-warden; for with men of contrarye Relligion I durst haue no conference. And haue send vnto your honours the names of all the Justices of peace of the two shyers within my dyocese, herin enclosed, with notes of Relligion, Learninge and wysedome bothe according to myne owne knowledge and that I by conference could learne, and lykwise the names of suche as in Relligion are syncere & favouringe the politie are most fytt men to be appoynted in place of some of the other. And as concerning other officers, in myne opynyon ther is nothinge that more hyndreth the good Successe of the policies estableshed nor dothe the perpetuall contynuaunce of the Sheriffwyke of Westmerland, by which meanes ther is allways suche in office as in no wyse favors the true way, and suche are suffered to passe through the countre vnapprehended as talke at their pleasure, and some haue in the wyld mountaynes preached in Chappells. The Quenes Receyvours and other officers of the lower sort, being not good them selfes, discourage often suche as darre not displease them. And to speake plainly to your honours, the noblemens tenauntes in this countre Darre not be knowen to favour that way for feare of losse of their fermholdes. And finally the Justices of Assyse which, only making a good face of Relligion in gevinge of the charge, in all other their talkes and dooinges shewe them selfes not favourable towardes any man or cause of Relligion, which the people moche marke & talke of. And thus according to my dewtie and the trust which your honours have putt in me, not fearing any man but setting god before myne eyes, I have doon my best endevours to avaunce the glory of god by yone, prayenge god to preserve the Quenes highnes in long healthe of bodye, contynuaunce of this good mynde and your honours harttes prepared of god to contynue in the diligent & most faythfull service of god and the Quenes maiestie as youe haue to your great praise begonne. Ffrom the Rose Castle in Cumberland the xviiith of November 1564.

Your honours most humble at comandment

JOANNES CARLIOLEN.[a]

f. 48a.

Justices of peace at this pointe viz. a° dni 1564 within the Countie of Cumberland, *scilicet*:

The bushoppe of Carlill, The Lord Dacre. My Lord Dacre, butt especially my Lady his wyfe, are to be reformed in Relligion.

Sir Thomas Dacre of Lannercost, Knight custos Rotulorum within the Countie of Cumberland, to be admoneshed in Relligion and verie vnfytt for that office.

Henrye Curwen of Workington, armiger, William Pennington of Muncaster, armiger, John Lampleugh of Lampleugh, armiger, Thomas Myddleton of Skyrwith, armiger, In Relligion good & meat to contynue & the said myddleton lerned somethinge in the Lawes.

John Aglionby of Carlill, armiger, Richard Blannerhasset; deade, armiger, not staid in Relligion but to be admoneshedd and within the lyberties of the Cetie of Carlill none other able but poore men.

Richard Salkeld of Corby or Rosgill, armiger, not good in Relligion.

William Myddleton, gent., William Pyckringe, gent., in Relligion evell & not meatt.

Justices to be appoynted at your honours election and pleasure for the said countie:

Henry Lord Scroope, Lord Warden, Mr. George Scroope, his brother.

[a] Best.

George Lampleughe of Cockermouth, armiger, Henry Towsone of Brydekyrk, armiger, Thomas Layton of Dalemayne, armiger, Mr. Anthony Twhattes of vnerigg, clerk, men of wysedome & good Relligion, experyent and lerned but not in the Lawes.

Thomas Carleton of Carleton, gent., Andrewe Huddlestone, gentleman, in Relligion good & wyttye men.

f. 48b.

Justices of peace at this pointe a⁰ dni 1564 within the countie of Westmerland, *scilicet:*

Sir Thomas Wharton of Whartone, knight, evill of Relligion.

Alane Bellingham, armiger, de Helsone lethes, Walter Streyckland de Syzer, armiger, Anthony Duckett de grarigg, armiger, all thre of good Relligion & meat men, and the said Bellingham lerned in the Lawe.

John Myddleton, gentleman, John Prestone, armiger, not of the shier, Richard Salkeld de Corkby & Rosgill, armiger, Oliuer Myddleton, gent., Richard Rigge, armiger, not good in Relligion, not fytt men.

Justices to be appoynted at your honours election and pleasure for the said countie :

Thomas Warcoppe de Smerdale, armiger, Lancelott Pyckring de Crosby Rawmwath,* armiger, Richard Dudley of Yenwath, armiger, Henry Crakenthorpe de Nebyging, armiger, William Gylping of Kentmyer, armiger, all verie good in Relligion & fytt men.

JOANNES CARLIOLEN.

f. 49a.

Glocestershire :

Myne humble dutie to your Lordships remembred, hauinge receaued your honorable Lettres dated the xvii[th] of this laste

* Ravensworth.

octobre, wherin yt pleased your Lordships to command me to consydre the state of my dyocesse touching th'obseruacion of lawes established for the ecclesiasticall pollicie and therof with others to certyfie your honors. It may please the same to be aduertysed that hauinge had conference with Sir Thomas Throckmorton, knight, Richard Pate, esquier, and others, touchinge the contentes of your Lordships lettres for the reporte of discorde in Justices of the peace and men placed in auctoritie, doo signifie vnto the same, that (god be praised) their are no Justices nor men placed in auctoritie within my dyocesse, eyther by them selfes disordered, or meynteyners of disordre in others, but have alwayes shewed them selfes redie to represse suche arrogansie and contempt of auctoritie as hath at any tyme bene offered before my beinge placed, and sythence very redie and willinge for myne assistance when nede hath required. I farther thinke there is nothing that bredeth at this tyme more vnquietnes and lesse credyt to the Quenes maiesties moste godly and honorable proceedinges then that some regard lytle or nothinge such ordre as is alredie established by the Quenes highnes ffor ecclesiasticall pollicie, whom I haue called and wylled to kepe ordre sett forth, but they contynue disordered as before, to whome lawe semeth to be no lawe & ordre no ordre. Ther is also a preacher, a man of great zeall & competent learninge, whom many of the countrie follow from place to place and receaue the communyon at his hand far from theire owne parisshes. I here men of good credyt, that he ys to populer in his sayenges, the redresse wherof I leaue to your Lordships wysedomes. The worshipfull of this countrie can certefie your honors further herein, yf they (f. 49b.) be required. Theise thinges I can rayther lament then amend and refourme, or geue your honoures so mete advise tendinge to the redresse therof as your greate wysedomes of your selfes can conceaue, beinge indede a man of smale experyence and lytle obseruacion in matters of pollicie & gouernmente; trystinge that your Lordships wyll take in good parte this my vnskylfull dealinge in these causes, for that I haue not bene traned therin and yet with all humblenes moste redie to doo mye dutie, so far as my poore knowledge wyll serue and as I shall be commaunded. Greate dysordre groweth of indyfferent thinges, which are in the appoyntment of the prynce, wherin I wyssh we might draw one waye, acceptinge them with oute supersticion or geuinge to lytle estimacion to auctoritie and ordre by which they ar established. I thinke also good to put your Lordships in remembraunce as well of wylliam Reade of Boddington and George Huntley of Fforocetor, esquiers, Late shrifes of this shire, to be placed agayne in commyssion of the peace, as also of John Hungerford, esquier, a man of worship and faire possessions, dwellinge moste communlie in this shire at Downe auney,[a] wher ther services in thoffice and Admynistracion of Justice ar verie nedefull as I here & as I thinke yt may therfore please your Lordships to consydre of them accordinglie; And so moste humblie takinge my leaue I commytt your Lordshipe to the tuycion of the almightie, who preserue you, from Gloucester the xx[th] of Novembre 1564.

  Your lordshippes most humble to commaund
           Ric. Glouc.[b]

  Endorsed: To the right honorable and my moste singuler good
    Lordes of the Quenes maiesties moste honorable preuye
    Counsell.
  f. 51a endorsed *ibid.*
  f. 52b endorsed *ibid.*
      Hast hast hast
      Hast with all diligence.
f. 53b.
  To the Quene her maiesties most honorable Pryvie Counoell.

f. 54b.
  My duetie in moste humble wise to your honors. Maie it please the same to be advertised that accordinge to your honors late requeste to be certified by me of the favorers and

---

[a] Atkins, p. 401, Amney.   [b] Cheyney.

mislikers of the present estate of religion, I have for aunswer
thereunto diligentlie conferred with Sir William Keilweye, Sir
Adrian Poyninges, Mr. William Vnedall, Mr. William Kyngesmill,
Mr. Richard Norton, Mr. William Jephsonne, Mr. James Pagett
and others of good religion. And for hable and meete menne
to be putt in commission for the peace besides those (that I
have hereafter noted to be favorers), I think vnder your honors
correction it shalbe verie expedient aswell that the sayd favorers
continewe in commission as that Mr. Thomas Carye, capitaine of the
Hurst Castle, Mr. William Bowyer of hambled(on) and Mr. Henrie
Clifford of Ffawleye were ioyned vnto them and also that by your
honorable wisdoms the Lordes herewith certified might be moved
to favor religion and to countenaunce the fautores and folowers
thereof. And the two younge Lordes, therle of Southampton and
the Lord Saindes, might nowe in there youthe be so trayned in
religion that hereafter when they come to there aucthoritie and
rule they shoulde not hinder the same. And because the citie of
Winchestre is moste noted in hampshiere either for good example or
evill (all that bear aucthoritie there except one or two beinge
addicte to thold supersticion and earnest fautores thereof), It should
be well donne to associate for the commission in the sayde citye
the Busshopp of Winton, Sir Henrye Seamour, William Vnedall,
henrye Wallopp, John ffoster and George Acworthe, the busshopps
chauncelour, and for hedd officers there, and in other tounes
fraunchised with Liberties, as Southampton, Basingstoke, Andever,
Romeseye, Petersfyelde and Portesmouth, Lymmington and Newport
in thisle of Wight and through the whole shiere, for cunstables and
bayliffes of hundredes and for generall enquestes by graund Juries
that by your honors Lettres earneste chardge and commandement be
given to the whole bodie of the commissioners and officers, that non
be appoynted vnto nor continue to exercise anie of the sayde offices
or callinges but they whose religion is approved, nor none likewise
placed or displaced by one or two, but by the common consent (of)

the benche at some generall session, which will easelie drawe the common p(eople) to one good conformitye when they in aucthoritie goe all one waye, or dothe not crosse or hinder the well doinges of another. As for Surrey, (by) reasonne of my smale continuance and lacke of acquayntaunce there, I (have) not vsed suche advise whearby throughlie to satisfie your honors but but (*sic*) partelie by credible reporte and partelie by myne owne knowledge have gathered this, and for incorporations, fraunchises, liberties and hundrede(s) within this shiere, suche ordere were good as is before mentioned for hamp(shire) as shalbe best consydered by your Lordshippes wisdomes, whome I praie almightie (God) Longe to prosper and maynteine in honorable estate to his glorie and government of his realme. ffrom ffarneham the xiii[th] daie of November a° 1564.

Your honorable Lordshippes moste humble to commaunde,

Rob. Winton.[a]

f. 54b., Col. a.

The Justices of peace in Hampshiere, Ffavorers:

The Busshopp of Winchester; Sir John Masson of Wintney; [Sir] William Pawlett; [Sir William] Keilwaye of Rockborne; [Sir] Henrie Seamer at Marwell; [Sir] Adrian Poyninges at Portesmouth; [Sir] John Barckeley at Christchurch; [Sir] Richard Pexall at stevington; [Sir] Oliver Wallopp at Ffarleighe; William Vnedall at Wykham; [William] Kingesmyll at Sydmanton; Richard Kingesmill, learned in the lawe; John Thornborough at ; Richard Gyfford at Kingesstunborne; Henrie Wallopp at ffarleighe; William Jephsonne at ffroyle; Richard Norton at Tistyd; Thomas Dearinge at Lysse; James Pagett at Burie; John ffoster at Badisleye;

Worsleye capten of thisle of Wight; George Milles in the wight; George Acworthe, doctor of the civill lawe, the bushopes chauncelor.

[a] Horne.

Mislikers or not favorers:

The Lord S⁺ John at Lettley (*sic*) castle; The Lord Chidiock Pawlett; William Pawlett of Vpelatford; William Bulckley at ffordyng-bridge; Robert Penrodocke of Charforde; Thomas Shelleye of Buryton.

John White of Southwirk, whoe notwithstandinge for skyll & his good administration of Justice maie is it veine so good to your honors continue still in the Commission (*sic*).

In the Citie of winchestre mislikers of religion of the chiefe aucthoritie.

Hodsonne the Maior; Bethell thelder and Bethell the younger; William Lawrence; White towardes the Lawe & Pottenger; Coreham towardes the Lawe and Skinner, Ffavorers.

Added at the side in Burleigh's hand:
Favorers in the Citie of Wynchester:
Colley; Brantor.

Col. b.
The Justices of Surrey, Ffavorers:
Mr. John Birche barron; [Mr.] Gilbert Gerard, atturnie generall; William Moore of Loseleye; Richard Onselowe of Cranleye; John Egmundsham of Hursleye; Thomas Browne of Biechworthe; Thomas Doile, stewerd to my Lord Caunturburies grace; William Bowyer of Camerwell.

Indifferent ministers of Justice within the countie of Surreye:
Sir Thomas Saunders of Cherl[wood]; Nicholas Lee of Adington; John Skinner of Rigat thelder; Nicholas Steydolf of Mickleham.

Gentlemen to be putt in commission of peace in Surreye:

Thomas Litle, keaper of Bagshott parcke; Thomas Dodmare dwelling aboute kea. . . . ; John Skinner the younger of Rigat; John Hurleston towardes the Lawe.

> Endorsed, f. 55 b: To the right honorable the Lordes and others of the Queenes maiesties privie Counsell.

f. 56.

Pleasith it your honorable estates to be advertised that after your Lettres directed vnto me for your informations what personagis maye be thought mete to be placed or contynued as Justices of the peace and who ought to be removed from the same, within my diocese and Jurisdiction of Canterbery, I haue the longer differred my answere for want of such sufficient Instructions as I laubored for to haue had. But concernyng the Countye of Kent I haue conferred with certen wise men therof. So that I haue gathered partly by myn owne knowledge and bi conference with others that these parsons in shedule inserted maye wel contynue to serue, with iii. others lastly named, of all which parsons though not of like zeale in religion yet such as I must saye that the furdest of[a] in fauorable affection toward the state of religion, be outwardly men conformable and not chargeable to my knowledge of any grete extremyties vttered bi them in afflicting the honest and godly, or in mayntenyng the perverse and ongodly, as your Letters do spcke.

Sir Thomas Wutton. Mr John tufton.

Thus trusting that I haue satisfied your honors request, I wysshe the same long preseruacion in grace and fauorable estate. Ffrom my house at Lamhith this xxiiiith of Novembre.

Your honors
MATTHUE CANTUAR.

[a] For "off."

f. lvii.

Percivallus Hart, Martinus Bowes, Willelmus Damsell, Henricus Cripse, Thomas Kempe, Georgius Howard, Thomas Cotton, Christopherus Aleyn, Henricus Cheyney, milites.

Thomas Wotton, Warhamus S^t leger, Richardus Baker, Johannes Cobham, Johannes Tufton, Thomas Scott, Willelmus Isley, Humfredus Hales, Willelmus Cromer, Johannes Lennard, Anthonius Weldon, Thomas Stanley, Thomas Asheley, Robertus Rudstone, Nicholaus Barham, Thomas Watton, Rogerus Manwood, Willelmus Lovelace, Johannes Meyney, Thomas Lovelace, Radulfus Bossevile, Georgius Darrell, Robertus Bynge, Thomas Doyley, Johannes Beere, Robertus Riches, Hugo Cartwright, Georgius Moulton, Georgius Ffame, Johannes Goldwell, Thomas Honywood, Thomas Hales, Hugo Darrell, Edwardus Boys, Gualterus Robertes, Nicholaus S^t. Leger.

f. 58.

Norfolk.

My bounden dutie vnto your honours humblie remembred, for answer of your honorable lettres receuid the xxviith of October and dated the xviith of the same, yt may like yow to be advertised that vppon conference and good advice taken with the duke of Norffolk his grace, Sir Edmund Windham, Sir Christofer heydon, Sir William Buttes, Sir Thomas Wodhowse, Sir Nicholas Lestrange knightes, the metest men in my opinion in this shire of Norffolk for this required seruice, by whose advice and certificat vnto me the Justices of peace of this Shire be verey well affected and geven to the executing of the orders and lawes of this Realme established for the ecclesiasticall policie, except Sir Thomas Lovell, Sir Thomas Tyndall,[a] knightes, Edmund Bowpre and M^r. Gybon of Lynne, Espuires, who are not thought by common fame to be so well bent as the other, yet I assure your honours, I know not of my part nor yet can lerne by anie probable meane, of anie fact that anie of them

[a] Sheriff, t. Eliz. Fuller's *Worthies*.

are to be charged with, and so leve it to your honorable consideracions. And for augmenting of the number of the Justices of this Shire, although there be divers mete parsons and well affected, yet considering (thankes be to god) the Shire being alredie in so good quiet with the advice of the above written persons I thinke the number sufficient for this Shire. And so leving to troble your honours I humblie take my leave, beseching god to send you much encrese of honour, ffrom Norwich this xviith of November 1564.
Your honours humble to commaund
JOHN NORWIC.[a]

f. 59.

It maye please your honours to be advertised that accordinge to the tenour of your honorable letters directed vnto me I haue sente herewithe, according to the forme in your said letters prescribed, a certificate in writinge, conteyninge the names as well of those Justices of the peace who are iudged not to be favourable to the ordinarie good proceadinges of the Realm in the ordres and causes of Religion, as also the names of those Justices that are well geven and meete to continue in office. And with all the names of some thought meete to be called to the said office. Of the which it may please your honours to haue suche consideracion as to your honorable wisdomes shall seme good. Thus ceassinge to trouble your honors, I humblie commend the same to the grace of god. Ffrom my house at Powles this xviith of November, 1564.
Your honorable Lordshippes
att Commandement
EDM. LONDON.[b]

f. 60.

Diocese London.—Ciuitas London.

The state and governement of the Cittye of London is allwaies subiecte vnto the eyes of your honors and therfore I haue not thought it greatlie necessarie to make anie reporte at this time of

[a] Parkehurst. [b] Grindal.

the governours therof being well ynoughe knowen, and in myne
opinion (as in suche a state) not to be misliked at this present.

f. 60 b.

Nomina Justiciariorum pacis 1564,
Middlesex.

Thomas Wrothe, miles, Edwardus Warner, miles, favourers of
godlie Religion.

Rogerus Cholmeley, miles, Martinus Bowes, miles, indifferent.

Thomas Chamberleine, miles, Thomas Sackeford, Master Requists,
Gabriel Goodman, Decanus christi, Gilbertus Gerrard, attorney
general, Willelmus Rosewell, sollicitor, Ricardus Onslow, recordator
Civitatis London, Robertus Nowell, attornatus Curie Wardae,
Johannes Asheldy, Edwardus ffitzgaret, Robertus Huycke, Petrus
Osborne, Edmundus Marten, Jasperus Ffisher, Tho. Wilson, legum
doctor, Robertus Chidley, Anthonius Stapleton, Johannes Newdi-
gate, all favourers.

f. 61 a.

Edwardus Bashe, I know not his Religion.

Johannes Marshe, Armigill Wade, favourers of Religion.

Edwardus[a] Randolphe, Indifferent, Henricus Iden, A favourer,
Robertus Harris, Indifferent, Rogerus Carewe, A favourer, Thomas
Elrington, not persuaded in Religion (as I am enformed), but in
his outwarde doinges semethe to me conformable.

Edwardus[b] Taylour,[c] Johannes Leake de Edmunton,[c] hinderers.
Christoferus Riche, indifferent.

Item, for the better governement of this Countie of Middlesex, it
is to be considered that sithens the death of Mr Hamondesham
there is never a Justice of the peace resient in the bodie of the
Shiere, for Mr Elrington liethe altogether in Surrey, Mr Newdi-

---

[a] Corr. from Barnardus.   [b] Corr. from Edūs.

[c] The Leakes of Edmonton occur as recusants in Middlesex Sessions Rolls
(County Records); also Edm. and Edw. Taylor.

gate moste parte in Buckinghamshiere, Mr Rithe (*sic*) moste commonlie at Lincolns Inne, Mr Carew, Mr Taylour and Mr Leake are in one extreme parte of the Shiere, the reste remaine about the Courte and about the Cittie: And yet for remedie herof I cannot hitherto finde owt anie apte men dwellinge in the harte of the shiere to exercise thoffice of Justice other then be alredie named.

f. 62a.

Nomina Justiciariorum Pacis in Comitatu Hartford.—Commorantium intra diocesem London.

Hartford:

Radulfus Sadler, [Radulfus Rowlet], milites, favourers.

Ricardus Lee[a] [miles], indifferent; Robertus Chester[b] [miles], an hinderer; Edwardus Caple [miles], indifferent but a verie good Justicer.

Alex. Nowell, decanus Sancti Pauli, Willelmus Barleye, Thomas Barrington, Georgius Gill, favourers.

Edwardus Bashe, *vide supra* in Middlesex.

Fraunciscus Walsingham, a favourer.

f. 62b.

Georgius Penruddocke, Willelmus Hide, favourers.

Georgius Hadley, Thomas Hauchet, Edwardus Taylor, hinderers.

Meete men to be put in the Commission of the peace in this Countie of Harford:

Mr Thomas Laventhorpe of Albery, esquier, a favourer; and William Hamond of Moudon gent., a favourer and skilfull in the Lawe.

Item, there is one Birkehead,[c] clerke of the peace in the said Countie, a notoriouse adversarie to religion of myne oun knouledge, and a great afflicter of the godlie and well disposed persones, whose removinge from that office (if it maye be lawfull) should do moche good.

[a] Got monastic property. Clutterbuck, iii., p. 7.
[b] A Sheriff. Fuller.
[c] Cor. from Dirkehead.

f. 62. (sic.)
Nomina Justiciariorum pacis, 1564. Besides the Lordes Counsellours & two Justices of the commone pleas.

Essex:
Robertus Riche, Anthonius Cooke, milites, favourers of Religion. Johannes Wentworth,ᵃ [miles], an hinderer.
Thomas Wrothe, Franciscus Jobson, Thomas Smythe, milites, favourers.
Thomas Goldinge, miles, indifferent.
Willelmus Bendlowes, Seruiens ad legem, an hinderer.
Thomas Sackeford, vnus magistorum curie Requistorum, favourer.
Thomas Mildmaye,ᵃ [Thomas] Powle, indifferent.
Willelmus Waldgrave, Thomas Lucas,ᵃ Kenelmus Throkmorton, Willelmus Aylife,ᵃ [Willelmus] Cardynall, Edwardus Barret,ᵃ Thomas Barrington,ᵃ Edwardus Berye, Johannes Tomworthe, favourers.

Comitatus Essex.

George Hadley, a hinderer ; Georgius Nicolles, favourer, learned in the lawe and to be trusted.

Jacobus Altham, indifferent. Edwardus Bockinge, George Christemas; these two in wordes seme to favour Religion, but are (as I am enformed) not favourable to the ministers of the same, and are besides noted to governe vndiscretlie, and insyncerelie, makinge gaine of the office, and this is affirmed to be true by divers graue and godlie persones of that countrey with whom I haue conferred.

Rogerus Amys, Clemens Syceley, favourers.
Willelmus Cheshull, an hinderer. Thomas ffranke, reported to be an hinderer, but in his wordes to me he hathe protested the contrarie; yf it be thought good he maye be tried for a time till I may searche owt the truthe more certeinlie.

Henry Goldinge, Edwardus Daniell, favourers.

ᵃ Sheriff. Fuller's *Worthies.*

f. 63.
ad huc Essex.

Johannes Wiseman, an hinderer; Mattheus Bradburie, indifferent; Edwardus Riche, favourer.

Men meete* in myne opinion to be putte into the Commission of the peace within the Countie of Essex which hitherto haue not bene in the Commission, viz.:

Mr Edward Isacke, Esquier, a favourer & of good truste; Mr John Moore, of Orsette, gentleman, a favourer skilled in the lawes and trustie.

Item, it is to be wisshed that one Jerome Songer, who moche afflictethe, vnder colour of arrerages of thexchequer bothe the poore ministers and also other simple people beyond good ordre, maybe vtterlie excluded from all directe and indirecte exercise of anie office vnder the Queues maiesty and namelie for anie recept of money or levieng thinges dewe to the prince.

f. 64.
Somersettshyre:

In most humble wise, as to dewtie appartayneth, it maie please your honors to be advertised that I vppon the sight of your Lettres concerninge the iustices of Peace wrote immediatelie to Sir Morrys Barckley, Sir Raff Horton and to Mr. John Horner to have their advice accordinge to the tenor of the same. And for further intelligens I have commoned with Justice Wealche, harry Portman, William Halley and John Hiperley, iustices, and can vnderstand nothinge of them, but that everie iustice in the shire of Somerset doo diligently (as they saie) exequute their offyce. I have not muche to saie against any man, but only by reporte, where with to trouble your honors I have not thought it good. I have hard good commendations of one Mr. John Carre, late of Bristoll, who nowe dwelleth in the said sheire in a place called Brent Mearsche, the Countrey there ys verie rewde and there ys

* Corr. from "might."

no Justice nighe save only Mr. Cuffer, who, for wante of healpe, ys not able to answere everie suyter, the said Mr. Carre I knowe to be wise, sobre, wealthie, and verie well affected to religion. There ys also commended one William Hyll of the Towne of Taunton, elder brother to Robert Hyll, one that ys well eastemed amonges his neighbours, and verie well knowen of all those that professe the Gospell, to be a sincere favorer thereof. There ys also one John Sydenham of Dulverton in the west parties of the said sheire, where there ys no Justice nighe, savinge Sir John Wyndham, who for age, sickenes and other cawses ys not nowe verie mete to doo service in that Offyce. The said John Sydenham ys well knowen to be wise, sobre and discrete, verie well affected to religion, a man well esteamed of his neighbours rounde aboute him. My humble suyte vnto your honors ys, that for the better performans of dewtie it might please youe to take Order, that every one that nowe ys, or hereafter shal be, called to the Office of a Justice, maie personallie take a solemne Othe before such as please your honors to appointe. And further if it be thought good to your honors, that they shall subscrybe their names to that Commission, that shall first be geven out to the Sheriff of everie Sheyre. I iudge verilie God shuld be better served, his worde more reverenced, the Quenes maiesties procedinges more humblie obeied, lesse grudge, and dowte amonge the common people, and so God fynallie, and on everie parte, most amplie glorified and all wee the Quenes maiesties most faithefull and humble subiectes bound to praie perpetuallie for her highnes longe and most prosperous raigne, and for your honors godlie successe in all your doynges durynge our Lyves. At London, this xxvii^t of Novembre Anno 1564.

    Your honors humble and dailie Orator,

        Gil. Bathe & Welles.[a]

Endorsed : f. 65 b.

 To the right honorable my verie good Lordes the Lordes of the Quenes Maiesties most honorable privey Councell.

      [a] Berkeley.

f. 66 a.

My singular good lordes for answer to your honorable letters of the xvii[th] of Octobre and received by me the xxv[th] of the same, may it please your Wisdomes to vnderstand thus muche. I have conferred Acording to your apointment with suche menne as hereafter be named in this schedule, concernyng such Justices as be in autoritie for their aptness to the same and favoring of religion and also for suche as be not placed and yet fitt for that place, and haue declared your honors their opinions severally as they send me theim in writing. And bicause it was your farther pleasure that I shuld declare severally my opinion also of suche other thinges that doe hynder these gudd procedinges, in the latter ende I have done it also. I wold have answered soner butt that they, dwelling farre of, did something prolong the tyme, and partly I my self have bene troubled with sickenes of late. Praised be the lorde of hostes that hais putt this zelous mynde in to the Quenes maiestie, [not onely to seke his glorie so zelouslye butt also to represse the hinderers of the same. And godd grant yor honors that contynuall ernest love of Justice, that thexeqution of suche godly lawes may be dulie practised and such good example come from you that the peple may be encoraged to doe the like. Thus with the commendation of my service I commend your honors to thalmightie, who for his vndeserved mercy sake long preserve her highnes and your honors to thadvancement of his glorie and cumfort of his peple. ffrom Aweland the xxii[th] of Novembre 1564.

Your honors most bounden & obedient
JA. DURESME.[a]

f. 68 a.

My Lord of Bedford sais that within his charge there is never a Justice of peace nor none that he can commend as mete for that purpose.

[a] Pilkington.

Sir John ffoster, Lord Warden of the mydell marche, thinkes these menne mete to be Justices and vsed in service.

Northumberland:
Cuthbert Lord Oyle, Sir Henry Percie, [Sir] John Witherington, [Sir] J. George Ratclif; Robert lawson, Cuthbert Horsley, skilled in the lawes; John Dalavell, George Heron, Nicholas Rydly, Cuthbert Carneby, Robert Mydelton, Sir Rauf Gray, Shiref vnder my Lord of Bedford, Sir Robert Ellercar he sais is a verie papist and all together vnlerned. He mislikes also Thomas Bates of Morpeth, and Sir John Mitforde of Highill he dowtes.

The towne of newcastell hais tenne aldermen, a maier and a shiref, everie alderman by their privilege is a Justice of peace as I here. they say that both theimselfes will be obedient to the lawes and kepe the towne so to with all their diligens, and surely if welth made theim not willfull both of their owne substance and the towne chamber by their impost of sea coole* it wold be one of the best townes on this side trent. The poorer sort hire theimselfes a precher butt none of theim or few gives litell or nothing to the precher.

Sir Robert Brandling, maior, Cuthbert Ellison, Bertram Anderson, Richard Hodshon, Christofer mytford, Oswold Chapman, Robert Ellison, Cuthbert Musgrave, John Wilkinson, William Dent, Robert Anderson.

f. 67 b.
In the Bishopricke of duresme, my Lord Evers and I think gudd to commend these Justices to your honors.

Charles, erle of Westmoreland, William Lord Ewrie, [William] Whittingam, deane, Sir George Bowes, Thomas Calverley, [Thomas] louton, lawers.

* Brand, *Newcastle*, ii. p. 269. The corporation was receiving £10,000 per annum from its duty on coal of 4d. per chaldron.

These other live quietly and obey the lawes:—Sir George Conyers, [Sir] William Bellasse, Robert Tempest, John Blaxston, Robert Swyfte, chancelor spirituall, William Hilton, Thomas Mydelton, Francis Bambrigge, Robert Bowes, Shiref, Christofer Chaiter, Gerrerd Salvyn, Edwerd Parkinson, William Smyth, Robert Lawson. John Swynborne kept a preist to say him masse butt he hais paid his fyne for it.

There be twoe other thinges in my opinion which hynder religion here muche. The Scottisshe preistes that are fledde out of Scotland for their wickednes and here be hyred in parisshes on the borders bicause they take lesse wages than other, and doe more harme than other wolde or colde in disswading the peple, I have done my diligence to avoide theim, butt it is above my power. The other thing is the grete number of scholers borne here about nowe lieng at lovan* without lycense, and sending in bokes and letters which cause many tymes evill rumors to be spredde and disquiet the peple. They be mayntened by the hospitals of the newcastell and the welthiest of that towne and this shire as it is iudged and be their nere cousins.

f. 69 a.

My humble duetie considered vnto your honors, whereas by your honors lettres I was commaunded to signifie vnto youe the names as well of those Justices of peace as of others, placed by anie meanes in auctoritie within my iurisdiction, whiche are not well affected to the moste godly state and order of theecclesiasticall policie of this Realme of England, But are rather of contrarie dispositions, and afflicters or at the leaste hinderers of the sayde ecclesiastical state, and that also I should certifie your honors of suche persons, who are well geven and meete to be called to office, withe theyre names and dwellinge places, These are to advertise your Lordships that I have, abowte this your will and commaundemente, conferred and vsed thadvise of the moste worshipfull and wiseste of my dioces,

* Louvain.

namelie Sir Peter Carewe, Sir John Chichester, Sir John Moore, Mr. Southcotte of Shillingforde, Mr. John Parker of Northmolton, Mr. John Carewe of Bickleye by Tiverton, who all withe good advisement and deliberacion gaue notice vnto me of suche persons, as well of thone to be displaced owte of office, as the other to be by the Queenes maiestie and your honors placed in office and auctoritie, whose names I haue written in the schedule heare inclosed, setting the names of the disfavorers of this case on the one side, and the names of the godlie affected on thother side and do moste humblie beseche youre honors to take in good parte this my shorte and rude answer vnto your Lordshippes lettres. And especiallie that youe will not be offended for that I haue not certified your honors withe suche expedition and convenient speede as youe required me. My onlie staye and Lette of no sooner answering was thexpectinge the returne of Sir Peter Carewe and Sir John Chichester from the vttermoste partes of Cornwall, where than they were, in exploitinge theyr diligence vpon certaine vrgente affaires of the Queenes highnes, and your honours commandemente, abowte vewing the portes of this whole countrie. And because it was verie Longe or they returned, I thought it good to suspend mine answer vnto your honors vnto suche tyme as I mighte vse theyr advises and counsels. Thus moste humblie submittinge my self vnto your honours, I committe the same to the tuition of Almightie god, who Longe preserue youe in most prosperous healthe and wealthe vnto his godlie will & pleasure, from Excestre the xxvi[th] of November 1564.

your humble suppliante to commaunde,
WILL. EXON.[a]

f. 70.

The names of suche Justices as were in the countie of Cornwall as in the countie of Devon, who are enemies or at the Leaste, no favourers of theecclesiasticall policie of this Realme.

[a] Alley.

Cornwall:

Inprimis, John Bevell,[a] Justice of peace, but a verie greate enemye. Item, [John] Polewheele, Justice, but an extreme enemie. Item, John Reskimer,[b] Justice, but an extreme enemy and an ill liver. Item, Richard Riskerocke, Justice, yet a Verie enemye.

The names of those whiche are meete to be Justices and to be called to office in the sayde Countie of Cornwall:

Inprimis, John Killigrewe the younger. Item, John Carminowe. Item, Nicholas [Carminowe]. Item, Richarde Trevanion. [Item], John Tralawine.[b] Item, Samson Mainton. Item, Richard Chaman. Item, John Anderton. [Item], Mr. Moyle of saint Germans.

Devon;

The names of those whiche are not counted worthie to be Justices in the Countie of Devon:

Inprimis, Marke Slader. Item, Christofer Copston, althoughe he be no enemie, yet he is not thoughte to be meete for the office of Justice by the reason of diuerse disorders. Other there be, who are not so earneste to mainteyne theecclesiasticall policie as they are wished to be, but yet for theyre Learninge, knowlege and wisdome they are thoughte meete men to continue in the saide office of Justice shippe.

The names of them who are counted meete to be placed in authoritie in the countie of Devon:

Inprimis, Mr. Edgecome.[c] Item, Mr. Butteshead. Item, Mr. John Carewe of Bickleye.

f. 70 b.

The names of those whiche are no Justices, yet being of some auctoritie are iudged no favorers of the foresaide state:

Inprimis, the greate Arundell[d] of Cornwall. Item, one Tregian

[a] Sheriff. Fuller.   [b] Sheriff. Fuller and Polwhele.
[c] Sheriff. Foller.
[d] Sir John Arundell of Lanherne. See Oliver's *Catholics*, p. 16.

of Cornwall. Item, one John Tremaine. [Item, one John] Tregudicke. Item, John Hill. [Item], William Cavill of Cornwall. [Item], Robarte Winter one of the Justices of the citie of Exeter. Item, one Harte, the towne Clerke of Exeter. [Item, one] ffleayre. [Item, one] Kirkham of Pinhowe by Exeter. [Item], other there be whiche are of a contrarie disposition but these be the chiefeste or at the leaste so counted.

The certificate of Thomas[a] Archbysshoppe of Yorke to the righte honorable the Lordes and others of the Queenes Maiesties moste honorable privie counsell. Towchinge and concerninge theyre lettres for Justices of peace within the Countie of Yorke and Cittye of Yorke parcelles of the diocese of Yorke.

Westrydinge:
Thomas gargrave, miles, Johannes Yorke, [miles], Richardus Corbett, Georgius browne, Henricus Savill, Thomas Waterton, Willelmus Lyster, Richardus Beamond, Richardus goodricke, Brianus Bayles, Willelmus Wombwell, Willelmus Swyfte, Hugo Savile, Johannes lambart, Junior, Willelmus tancard, ar(migeri), Justices that be favorers of Religion.

Westrydinge:
Willelmus Vavasour, miles, [Willelmus] Ingleby, [miles], vicecomes, Thomas Danby, Willelmus Mallory, Milites, Frunciscus Woodrofe ar., Edwardus Elltoftes ar. Necessarye men, frunciscus Palmes, ar., Willelmus Hamond, ar.; Willelmus Hungate, [ar.], Johannes Lacye of Cromwel bothom, Henry Gryce ar., Justices that be no favorers.

Westrydinge:
ffrunciscus slingesbye, Richardus Malwerey, Robertus Lee,

[a] Young.

Johannes Beverley, Richardus Asheton, R[ichardus] Buny, ar[migeri], men meete to be Justices of peace & favorers.

Estrydinge :
Thomas gargrave, miles, henricus gate, miles, Johannes Vaghan, Christoferus Estofte, Henricus Savile, Johannes Eglesfyld, Thomas Eyuns, Christoferus Hylliard, Willelmus Strickeland, Anthonius Smethlecy, Radulfus counstable de sepulcres, Thomas Boyneton, ar[migeri], Justices that be favorers of Religion.

Estrydinge :
Willelmus Babthorppe, miles, a Justice of peace & no favorer of religion.

Estrydinge :
John Counstable, Knight, Symon Musgrave, George Dakyns, Arthur [Dakyns], Bartholomewe Abbott, ar[migeri], meete to be Justices of peace & favorers.

f. 72a.
Northrydinge :
Thomas Gargrave, miles, Nicholaus ffayrefaxe, [miles], Henricus gate, [miles], Georgius Bowes, [miles], Rogerus Dallton, Roger Ratclyf, Johannes Herbert, Walterus Strickland, Thomas Layton, Willelmus Davell, Averedus Vnedall, ar[migeri], Justices and favorers of Religion.

Northrydinge :
Christoferus Danbye, miles, Leonardus dacre, Thomas Rookeby, Johannes Sayre, Machaell Wandesfurth, Anthonius Catteracke, ar[migeri], Justices and no favorers of Religion.

Northrydinge :
Christoferus Metcalfe, miles, Willelmus tancard, Thomas Gower, Thomas Savile, Robertus Barneton, Radulfus Bowrchyer, ar[migeri], meete to be Justices & favorers.

Justices of peace within the Cittie of Yorke :
James Sympson, maior, Robertus Hall, Thomas Apleyard, Robertus Hekleton, Johannes Bone, Willelmus Cowpland, [Willelmus] Beckkewh, Robertus Pecocke, Thomas Staneven, Thomas Lawson, Percyvall crayforth, Justices & no favores of religion.
Willelmus Wattson, Radulfus Hall, Justices there & favorers of Religion.

f. 73 a.
The certificat of Thomas Archbysshoppe of Yorke to the righte honorable the Lordes and others of the queenes maiesties privie Counsell towchinge & concerninge theire lettres for Justices of peace within the countie of Nottingham parcell of the diocese of Yorke.

Comitatus Nottingham, Justices of peace there and favorers of religion:
Sir John Herrsye, knight, [Sir] William Meringe, [knight], Robert Markeham, esquier, John Byron the younger, George Nevill, Bryan Stapleton, William Burnell, [esquiers], Justices of peace there and no favorers of religion.

Comitatus Nottingham predictus :
Sir Gervys clyfton, knighte, Sir John Byron [knighte], bothe good subiectes & necessarie for service in theire countrie but in religion vearie cold.

TO THE PRIVY COUNCIL, 1564. 73

Sir Anthony Styrrley, [knight], [Sir] William Hollys, [knight], John Mannors, esquier, Thomas Stanhoppe, esquier, Ffrauncis Mullenax, esquier, nowe sheryf, Gabriell Barewicke, [esquier], Nicholas Powterell, [esquier], sargent at lawe.

f. 80.

Chester:

This cittie is governed bie xxiiii^{ty} Aldermen, out of which Nomber the Maior is yerelie chosen, who immediatlie apon his othe taken is a Justice of peace and so after Continueth duringe his lief and albeit the graunte of their Charter is so ample that neither Alderman nor Justice of peace can be displaced, yet I have signified who be favorers, who be not, and who be most mete bothe for zeale and habilitie to be made Aldermen as any Rowme shall fall.

Justices favorable:

Laurence Smith, knight, William Gerrard, Esquier, John Websbow, Henry Hardware, Raffe Goodman senior, John Cowper.

Justices not favorable:

Richard Poole maior, William Sneide, knight, John Walley, John Smith, Thomas Smithe, John Offley, William Aldersey, Randle Bamvile.

Col. 1.

Aldermen not Justices yet favorable:

Richard Harper, armiger, sergeant at law, William Leche senior, Adam Goodman, Morris Williams, Thomas Grene.

Col. 2.

Aldermen not Justices neither favorable:

Randle Manwaringe, Roberte Walley, Roberte Johns, Raffe Goodman.

Col. 3.

Meete to be Aldermen for their zeale and habilitie :
Richard Sutton, William Hanmet, Henry Leche, John ffisher, Oliuer Smithe, Edward Marten, Edward Hanmer, John Hankie, Christopher Morvile, William Crofton, John Yerworthe.

ff. 81-83 are here arranged in tabular form to save space.

In the original the names are arranged in three columns under the hundreds or parcells.

f. 81.

Countie Chester.

	Justices favorable.	Not favorable.	Meete to be Justices.
Hundred de Eddesbury	John Savage de Clifton knight Raffe Dent de Vtkinton, armiger	John Bryne de Stapleford, armiger	George Bieston de Bieston, armiger Richard Birkenhed of Manley, Gentlemen Learned in the Lawe
Hundred de Bulkley	Raffe Leycester de tofte, knight	John Dutton of Dutton, armiger	Richard Brooke de Norton, armiger, Thomas Leighe de Leighleighe, armiger John Grinnsdiche de grinnsdiche, armiger, Learned in the Lawe
Hundred de Macclesfield	Edward Ffitton de Gawswerth, knight	Henricus Bierton de hanford, knight William Davenport de bromhall, knight Roberte Tatton de Withenshawe, armiger Piers Leighe de Lime, knight John Warren de Pomton, armiger	Thomas Stanley de Wever, armiger Richard Sutton de Sutton, armiger Raffe Arderne de Hardeine, armiger William Dokenfield de Dokenfeld, armiger Jaspar Worthe de Dittrington, armiger

LETTERS FROM THE BISHOPS

	Justices favorable.	Not favorable.	Meete to be Justices.
Hundred de Nauntwich	Laurence Smith de Houghe, knight John Delves de Aington, armiger	Non to my knoledge	John Mushull de Mushull, armiger Edmond Griffin de Bartherton, armiger Roberte Vernam de armiger
Hundred de Northwiche	Non to my knoledge	Thomas Venables de Kinderton, knight	Henry Manwaringe de caringham, armiger Charles Manwaringe de Croxton, armiger William Liversage de Whelock, armiger
Hundred de Broxon	Hugh Cholmondley de Cholmondley, knight George Calveley de Ley, armiger Richard Hurleston de Pickton, armiger	Non to my knoledge	Richard Clyve de Huxley, armiger
Hundred de Wirrall	Richard Houghe de Leighton, armiger William Glastor, armiger	William Massie de Podington,* armiger, a good Justice	John Poole de Poole, armiger

* Sheriff. Fuller's *Worthies.*

f. 82.   COUNTIE LANC'

	Justic favorable.	Not favorable.	Meete to be Justices.
Hundred de Lonsdale	Thomas Carus Sergeaunt, ar'	Francis Tunstall de Thurland, ar'	Non to my knoledge
Hundred de Amoundernes	Thomas Calvert de Sokerham, ar'	George Browne de Ribchester, ar' Richard Shirburne de Stannehurst, k' John Rigmaiden de Garstoinge, ar'	Non to my knoledge
Hundred de Blagburne	Non to my knoledge	John Sothworth [a] de Sampsbury, k' John Osbaldeston de Osbaldeston, ar' John Townley [a] de Townley, ar' Richard Ashton de Whalley, ar' John Bradill de Whalley, ar'	Giles Parker de Harropforth, gent Brian Parker, gent, learned in the lawe
Hundred de Leyland	John Fletewodde de Penwortham, ar'	Thomas Hesketh de Rusforth, knight Edward standish de standishe, ar' Hugh Anderton de Yexton, ar'	Thomas Ashall de Hill, ar' [b] Thomas Butlour de Bewsay, ar'

[a] Harland, p. 70, conformable.   [b] Above scratched out Thomas Stanley de Winweke.

	Justic favorable.	Not favorable.	Meete to be Justices.
Hundred de Derby	John Atherton de Atherton, knight	Richard Molinex de Sefton, knight Henry Halsall de Halsall, ar' Laurence Ireland de lideate, ar'	Thomas Stanley de Winweke, knight
Hundred de Saulgeford	Edward Holland de denton, ar' Edmond Ashton de Chatterton, armiger	William Radcliffe de ordishall, knight Roberte Barton de Smethelles, ar' Ruffe Ashton de Leyver, ar'	Thomas Herle, gardian of Mancester Edmond Trafford de Trafford, ar' Charles Ratcliffe Todmerden, ar' Richard Ratcliffe, gent, of xx[ti] Landes, zealous and wise John Asheton, Clark, zealous and learned

f. 83.

The Archdeaconrye of Richmonde is in my Jurisdiccion Conteyneth in hit diuerse Parcelles of sundrie Countries, viz.:—

	Justic favorable.	Justic not favorable.	Mete to be Justic.
Parcell of the Countie York wherein be theis Justic	Walter Strickland de Crofte, ar' John Saier de Merske, ar' Avery Vnedalle de Merick, ar'	William Tankard de borrobrigge, ar' Christopher Danbie de Well, knight Machaell Wandisfurth de Pickall, ar' Theis be good Justic altho not very favorable William Inglebie de Ripley, knight Richard Norden de Wath, ar' Christopher Wivell de Masham, ar' William Wicliffe de Wicliffe, ar' Antony Caterick de stanwick, ar' Antony Rokby de Rokbie, ar'	Roger brough de brough, ar' William Peper de Richmond, gent Roberte Heblethwaite, commissary of my Archdeaconry of Richmond
Parcell of the Countie Cumberland wherein be theis Justic	William Pennington de Moncaster, ar'	Henry Curwen de Workington, ar' John Lampluffe de Lampluffe, ar'	Non to my knoledge

	Justic favorable.	Justic not favourable.	Mete to be Justic.
Parcell of the Countie Westmoreland wherein be theis Justic	Alane Bellinghame de Kendall, ar'	John Middleton de lonsdale, ar' Antonie Duckett de Kendall, ar' Theis be good Justic altho not very favorable Oliuer Middleton de Bithonie, gent	William Gilpen de Kentmaire, ar'
Parcell of the Countie Lanc' wherein be theis Justic	Non to my knoledge	Antony Kirkby de Kirkbie, ar' A good Justic	John Preston of ffornes, ar'

f. 84 b is endorsed To the right honorable the Queens Maiesties Privie Counsell. On the remaining folios numbered xci-xcvi the lists of "mislikers" and of men fit to be justices are again copied out.

f. 97 (unnumbered).

Syr, I send your honor the namys of such as be commended to me in these shiers; what these be & what others be, your honors of the councell knowe moche better than we can enforme youe, and as for myself, I know them not and somtyme enformers serve ther own turne & gratifie ther frendes.

As for bristowe diocesse the commendatory therof shuld haue sent his certificat. thus Jesus be with your honor,

Yours euermore
Matthue Cantuar.

In the dioces of Landaff:
Glamorganshire.
Sir George Herbard, M^r. Edward Manxell, [M^r.] Roberte Gamage, [M^r.] Edward Lewes, [M^r.] Tho. Lewes, [M^r.] Myles Buttin, comes, William Evans, chancellour, Christopher Turberfeild, M^r. Dauid Evans of North, M^r. Lesam price [M^r.] William Jenkin.

Momworthe Shire.
The Erle of Worceter, M^r. Tho. Mawgan, [M^r.] Charles Somerset, [M^r.] Tho. Herberd, [M^r.] William John stroger, [M^r.] Evans, Chauncellour.

In the dioces of Oxford :
Sir Tho. Benger, knight, Henrye Nores, Esquier, M^r. Wayman, [M^r.] fynes, [M^r.] John Doyly, [M^r.] Roberte [Doyly,] [M^r.] Tho. Wynchecombe, [M^r.] Gibbons, [M^r.] Cowper, [M^r.] Moore, Mr. Lea, [M^r.] Davas, Ambros Dormer.

Justices of peax in the Citie Oxon :
Doctor White, [Doctor] Warner, M^r. Todde, Mrs Taverner, Denton, Brostrun, Charelton, Croker, Rawlyns.

Endorsed: To the right honorable Sir William Cecyll, knight.

Then follows an index of dioceses & counties: thus f. lxxxv. (*sic*) :—

		Comitatus.	
Bath & Welles		Somerset	f. 64
Carlile		Cumberland	48
		Westmoreland	48
Canterbury		Kent	57
Chichester		Sussex	7
Chester		Chester	80-81
		Lancaster	82
	parcell	Yorkshire	83
	of	Westmoreland	83
Coventry &		Derby	41
Lichfield		Stafford	40
		Salop	42
		Warwick	43
Duresme		Northumberland	68
Ely		Canterbridge	16
Exeter		Devon	70
		Cornwall	70
Glowcester		Glowcester	49
Bushops of		Hereford	9
Hereford		Salop	10
		Wigorn	11
		Radnor	11
		Monmouth	12

Lincoln	Lincoln	20-21
	Bedford	22
	Huntington	22
	Herts	23
	Leicester	24
	Bucks	26
London	Middlesex	61
	Essex	63
	Herts	62
Norwich	Norffolk	58
	Suffolk	46
Peterborough	Northampton	31
	Rutland	32
Sarum	Wiltshire	35
	Berks	36
Winchester	Southampton	54
	Surrey	54
Wigorn	Worcester	2
	Warrick	3
York	Yorkeshire	71
	Nottingham	73

Then follow 3 endorsements of letters to the Privy Council & the volume concludes:

"Collection of original letters of divers Bishops sent to the Privie Councill in the beginning of the Reigne of Q. Elizabeth & certifying the names of persons qualified or disqualified for the Commission of the Peace, as they are affected or disaffected to thestablished Religion.   A° 1564."

INDEX TO DIOCESES.

Bath & Wells	pp. 63-64
Carlisle	48-51
Canterbury	57-58
Chester	73-80
Chichester	8-11
Coventry & Lichfield	39-47
Durham	65-67
Ely	23-26
Exeter	67-70
Gloucester	51-53
Hereford	11-23
Llandaff	81
Lincoln	26-33
London	59-63
Norwich	47-48 & 58-59
Oxford	81-82
Peterborough	34-37
Salisbury	37-39
Winchester	53-57
Worcester	1-8
York	70-73

PAPERS

RELATING TO

THOMAS WENTWORTH,

FIRST EARL OF STRAFFORD.

FROM THE MSS. OF DR. WILLIAM KNOWLER.

EDITED BY

C. H. FIRTH, M.A.

PRINTED FOR THE CAMDEN SOCIETY.

M.DCCC.XC.

www.ingramcontent.com/pod-product-compliance
Lightning Source LLC
Chambersburg PA
CBHW032249080426
42735CB00008B/1068